Europe on a
G-String

Europe on a G-String

for summer lovers everywhere .....

L. A. Florrie

To order additional copies of this book, contact:
Xlibris
AU TFN: 1 800 844 927 (Toll Free inside Australia)
AU Local: 0283 108 187 (+61 2 8310 8187 from outside Australia)
www.Xlibris.com.au
Orders@Xlibris.com.au
817140

This book is dedicated to everyone who has a story to tell.

Dedicated also to Mum and Dad, for guiding and watching over me from above. I love and miss you both so much.

ACKNOWLEDGEMENTS

Thanks to my wonderful partner, Steve, aka Carlo, for your unwavering love and support in all that I do. Thank you also for being my second pair of eyes and for helping me with all the technical stuff. I love you heaps. Q.

Thanks to my sisters, Elizabeth and Kelly for your support and encouragement. I love you guys, you're the best. To the rest of my family, I love each and every one of you.

Thanks to Brooke, Claire and Emily and to all our friends and lovers in this book, you know who you are. It was fun.

Thanks to Rudolf, for motivating me to look at things differently.

Huge thanks also to Cherry, Jonah and all the wonderful team at Xlibris, for always being there when I had so many questions. Your assistance has been invaluable. Thank you for your professionalism, care and patience.

INTRODUCTION

A Little Bit about Your Travel Companions

Brooke

B ROOKE WAS BORN in Queensland, Australia, to Margo, a funny, robust, intelligent, and well-read woman from the north-west of England. As a young, 21-year-old woman in post-war Britain, Margo was desperate to escape the doom and gloom. The miserable weather played a huge part in her wanting to leave the UK. Besides, none of her friends ever had the desire to do anything or go anywhere other than to get married, have kids, and move no farther than a few houses or streets away. Her family was devastated that she wanted to pack her bags and head off into the unknown, but for Margo, it was time to start a new life elsewhere. Adventure for Margo was beckoning.

Having been obsessed with all things Hollywood for most of her life, Margo tried her luck with America but sadly was rejected, the American Embassy suggesting she try Canada, New Zealand, or Australia instead. Margo's brother Tom, a merchant seaman, told her to head down under as he'd heard it was a country that offered many opportunities; plus, the weather was hot. With Tom's recommendation in mind, she applied to the Australian Embassy, her application was approved, and she jumped on a ship to Brisbane, along with other British escapees as ten pound poms where, upon arrival, all passengers were relegated to living in the quintessential, no-frills migrant hostel.

Margo loved Australia from the get-go, despite enduring the relentless bouts of homesickness complaints and whines of regret from many of the resident immigrants. Not allowing herself to be dragged into the depression of those yearning for the motherland, Margo headed south to the Gold Coast, where she encountered the local hustler who charmed his way into her life. She was told by the local priest to steer well clear of him, but not one to be told what to do and liking her potential beau even more because of his reputation, Margo dated him anyway. They later married, with Margo giving birth to her very own Hollywood cast; and in order of appearance came John, Brooke, Joe, and Peter.

Margo was one of the funniest women ever and had an answer – and always the correct answer, I might add – to every question put to her. Brooke inherited many of Margo's traits. She was funny, a great storyteller, intelligent, gorgeous, and impetuous. Brooke also inherited a few of her father's traits. She was smooth, a sweet talker, and charming.

Margo made sure that her home was filled with love and fun, ensuring that all who visited were provided with great entertainment and plenty of food and drink. Life was never dull at Margo's place, with the whole family vying to be the best joker and storyteller. The hours there had no meaning, with no clock on the wall to suggest it was time for last orders. It was often a surprise to all to be told it was three o'clock in the morning, with the party still in full swing and showing no signs of slowing down or of anyone wanting to go home. Margo and her family were a tightly knit clan. They were all highly intelligent and well-read people.

Brooke was loved unconditionally by her family, and in many ways, she was Margo reborn, desperate to escape her boring job on the Gold Coast and travel to the other side of the world. Margo saw herself in Brooke and totally understood her daughter's passion for fun and adventure and encouraged her 100 per cent. Brooke's love for life was contagious, and everyone flocked to her like a moth to a flame. She was forever happy and optimistic, never letting anything get her down, the kind of gal pal you need by your side when the going gets tough.

Brooke's upbringing was similar to mine in many ways, and it was destiny's collision course that brought us together for a lifetime of indubitable, watertight friendship. Having lived and worked in many countries over the years, Brooke eventually returned home to the Gold Coast, where she currently lives with her husband and gorgeous family.

Claire

Claire was born in Sydney and was 5 years old when her parents moved the family up to the Gold Coast in Queensland. Claire's father, an academic, had accepted the role of principal at a local school, ensuring a stable future for them all. Claire's parents were quite conservative and community-minded. With the family happily ensconced in their sea change, providing a completely new lifestyle, Claire's mother continued to immerse herself in various charity organisations, also helping out at the local church op shop.

Claire did really well at school and passed all her subjects with top marks. She was studious, sweet, and a fairly quiet child. She was also a born worrier.

Life at home for Claire was supportive and nurturing, albeit regimented and orderly. She and her slightly older brother, Luke, went to the local church dance every Friday night, accompanied by their mum, who would vet every male Claire came into contact with. It was a different story where Luke was concerned, however, his mum pushing him into dancing with as many girls as she could muster.

Luke also excelled at school and became the captain of the school cricket team. He never seemed interested in girls, preferring to hang out with his cricket mates. There were rumours that he was gay, but no one ever really knew, not then. His parents ignored the signs, instead choosing to invite some of the nicer girls from church to tea, hoping he'd take the bait. He never did, and Claire always felt sorry for him. Luke respected his parents and knew that it would be difficult for them to completely approve of his lifestyle, but he bravely and officially came out to them at the age of 23. They weren't shocked, of course, even though it still took them time to accept who he was.

Claire looked up to her much older sister, Susan, whom she adored. Susan, being twelve years older, however, didn't have much in common with Claire but loved her all the same. Susan was a librarian. Claire would often sit with Susan when her parents were out. Even if Susan was busy reading or sewing, Claire just loved being in her company, not saying a word.

Devastatingly for Claire, Susan flew the coop as soon as she met Fredrik, a good-looking and nicely mannered man from Norway. Fredrik, who was backpacking around the world, had been travelling through Australia when he and Susan had literally bumped heads on the pavement outside the post office. He'd been in to buy some stamps, dropping his wallet on the way out. Susan was walking towards Fredrik, and watching the scene unfold before her, had rushed in to pick it up for him just as he bent down at the same time, and – voila! – it was pretty much love at first sight, and so their Nordic story began. Claire said that Susan loved to tell the story of how they met. Fredrik whisked Susan away from all that she knew back to Norway, and Claire worried about her and missed her dreadfully.

Claire met Brooke through a work colleague, and they formed a close relationship. I suppose, in a way, Brooke had become a surrogate sister to Claire, and it was during their friendship that Claire assimilated some of Brooke's more unreserved ways, with a small part of Brooke's vivacious and bubbly personality rubbing off on her. From what I had heard about Claire's earlier years, I certainly didn't place the old Claire with the new and improved version.

When Claire heard of Brooke's and my plan to go to Europe, she was in like Flynn. This was her opportunity to also escape her boring, rigid life and have some real fun. Not putting too fine a point on it, I suspected she also had her own underlying plan evolving as a way to eventually get to Norway to be reunited with her sister again. All was well in Claire's world.

Claire is now happily married to the man of her dreams. They have three wonderful children, and all live in Brisbane.

Emily

Emily was born and raised on the Wirral, a metropolitan borough of Merseyside, to middle-class parents. Emily's mum and dad were both teachers as was her elder sister Sarah. James, Sarah's husband, also taught at the local school. Her other sister, Jane, was a nurse. Their mum taught special needs kids, and their dad similarly taught kids with severe disabilities, building the first ever youth club for them.

Emily's dad was an incredible campaigner and fundraiser and was awarded an MBE for all his charity work, something the whole family were proud of and were able to take part in. Her dad was also a great musician, and there was always music being played at home. Emily admired her dad's charity work and, in his footsteps, now sits on the board of a music therapy charity.

Even though Emily's parents were teachers, they weren't terribly strict with her. Emily was the youngest, after Sarah and Jane, and was the comic of the family, always playing practical jokes and causing havoc in the household. She would often shimmy down the tree outside her bedroom window late at night to go out with her friends, leaving her pillows perfectly moulded under the sheets in the shape of her young schoolgirl body. Emily's mum and dad were never any the wiser.

Emily didn't have to work hard at school. She had a ridiculously high IQ at a young age and was far too bright for her own good. She was a very talented musician, like her dad. Emily played violin in the national youth orchestra, so she was often able to swap school lessons for concerts, which gave her the freedom she loved from a young age and which set the tone for the rest of her life.

Sadly, when Emily was 12, her parents had a three-year separation. Emily went to live with her mum, and Jane stayed with her dad, while Sarah and James lived their own separate lives, continuing with their teaching and raising a family. Emily was close to her mum, and they had a lot in common.

Emily's mum had a great sense of humour, which she inherited from her dad, who worked for a huge global entertainment conglomerate bringing cinema to the north of England. Emily's mum was fortunate enough to have attended many premieres with her dad and met some wonderful film stars, so it wasn't surprising that Emily ended up living in Los Angeles for a while, attending the Oscars on more than one occasion.

Emily's mum also had a great sense of style and loved the finer things in life, taking Emily on amazing holidays to unusual places, the two of them composing and singing songs together as they journeyed life's path. At the ripe old age of 13, Emily's first overseas trip with her mum was to North Africa, which awakened her love for travel. As wonderful as life was with her mum, they were also extremely difficult years for Emily as she struggled to live without her dad and her two sisters in their huge family home, like it once was.

To know and appreciate Emily is to be enlivened by her charm and fun persona, her spontaneity, and her love for total freedom. To date, she's lived in eight different countries and has worked in many more since we met back in 1980. Emily is currently single, although, knowing her, probably not for long. She lives in London with her gorgeous dog, Scout.

But more about each of these wonderful characters in the following pages and some stuff about me as I put fingers to keyboard, recalling some of our most amazing memories. So join us as we set off on our unforgettable journey.

CHAPTER ONE

B ROOKE WAS LATE again. After weeks of plotting and scheming, surely it wasn't too much to expect that she'd arrive on time just this once? I mean, seriously, it wasn't like we were waiting for her at the local supermarket to buy the weekly groceries, a chore way down on her list of things to do. We were at Brisbane International Airport for crying out loud, the place where it was all about to begin – our European adventure. Brooke was one of the greatest enthusiasts the world had ever known, but her aversion to good timekeeping was well-documented. She loved many things in life, but the one thing she loved above all else was being at an airport, any airport, sitting in the departure lounge, gin and tonic in hand, waiting to board a flight to anywhere. Her face would light up the darkest room at the very thought of travelling to some exotic far-off, distant place to indulge in gay abandon. It meant freedom, excitement, new horizons, new men. So where was she, today of all days?

The terminal was frenetic with zillions of people coming and going, each of them immersed in their own personal thoughts of life's journey ahead. I was immediately caught up in the parade of globetrotters, ecstatic that I, too, was now part of the jet set. *Wow, it's really happening,* I confirmed to myself, my pace quickening from sheer exhilaration. There were singles and couples and groups and families and business people, and I'd never seen so many backpackers collectively in one place.

Maybe I should've bought myself a backpack, I thought, enviously observing the ease at which these uncomplicated travellers negotiated themselves and their belongings through the crowd.

At the very least, I could've treated myself to a suitcase with wheels, I told myself as I sat down to inhale the excitement. I looked down at my dented old blue suitcase and sighed. It had certainly seen better days, but we'd been faithful holiday companions over the years, and it just didn't seem fair to trade it in for a newer model. Adorned with stickers from our many travels together, its maturity and unique appearance deserved my respect. It was a special suitcase – a suitcase that never failed to take care of my possessions, a suitcase that held within it fragments of unforgettable memories, a loyal suitcase. I smiled as I recalled some of the more memorable vacations we'd shared. I lugged my old friend with renewed vigour.

The voice over the loudspeaker was busily announcing arrivals and departures. Names were being called, prompting a wave of panic as late holiday-goers made last-minute dashes to departure gates. I couldn't help but notice their pale, albeit energised, physiques as each second took them closer to their sun-drenched destinations. The dispirited arrivals of the bronzed and bleached, noticeably united in their post-holiday blues, was a clear sign that the good times were over for them for at least another year, until their next two-week vacation. I felt the emotion of loved ones saying goodbye, and I smiled as others were reunited. My heart was racing as the adrenaline deep within me soared. Airports never failed to excite, and today was no exception.

Claire and I had arrived within seconds of each other, each with our very own entourage of farewell committee members in tow. We hugged excitedly. Claire looked radiant, her face flushed with euphoria. Donned in long white pants, a pink twin set, and pearls, she looked as pure and wholesome as ever. Her shoulder-length light brown hair framed her pretty face, and her green eyes were glistening, her trademark sweet pink lipstick forever enhancing her heart-shaped lips. 'Can you believe it?' she gushed. 'After everything we've talked about and planned for, today's the day!'

'I know, Claire. I feel like I'm about to explode with excitement,' I replied with equal elation.

Claire's eyes scanned the crowd. 'Typical of Brooke not to be here on time. Three times I reminded her of our rendezvous time last night, *three* times!'

'So stop worrying then,' I said firmly. 'She'll be here.'

Claire didn't seem convinced.

'Well, I guess now is as good a time as any for the essentials check,' I said, quickly steering the subject away from our missing traveller.

Claire opened her handbag and proudly flaunted one newly printed, hot-off-the-press passport, one ticket to paradise, and a wad of money in her wallet. 'Do you know how many times I've checked my bag this morning, making sure I had the three vitals?' She laughed. She asked me the same question.

'Check number fifty coming up,' I gibed, opening my handbag. I, too, delighted in brandishing one current passport, one valid ticket to utopia, and enough money for my one-way trip.

'Ta-da!' I crooned. We hugged again, pure joy running through our veins. We made ourselves comfortable on the lounge chairs and discussed our imminent adventure.

My sisters, Elizabeth and Kelly, had come with me to the airport to say their goodbyes, and Claire had brought her mum and brother, Luke, with her as convoy. Twenty minutes had passed, and Brooke was still nowhere in sight. Claire was drifting away from the fun conversation the rest of us were having. I knew she was preoccupied with the absence of Brooke. I wondered, too, for a minuscule of a second where she was. *We can't leave without her. Or can we?* I asked myself. The minutes ticked by, and the idea of a holiday without her would be like Charlie operating without the third angel.

'I'm beginning to think she *really* isn't coming,' lamented Claire, scrutinising her watch with that concerned look of hers we all knew so well. Claire always went into worry mode when Brooke didn't show up on time.

Please make Brooke arrive in the next few minutes, I appealed silently to the universe on Claire's behalf.

The thing was, though, Brooke never wore a watch, which made it pretty much impossible for her to *ever* arrive on time. She never meant to keep people waiting as she loved nothing more than catching up with friends for lunch or wild nights out on the town. She was the life and soul of any gathering and a big-time social junkie. Everyone adored Brooke, and to all who truly knew her, it was a given that she invariably ran behind schedule. Her belated entrance would always be accompanied with a profuse apology, but it was never her acknowledgement of remorse that absolved her; it was her smile. She just had the most dazzling smile with perfectly straight white teeth. The world could end at any minute, but if Brooke flashed that smile of hers, it was a sure thing we'd all live to see another day. 'You should be in a toothpaste commercial,' I used to tell her.

'She'll be here soon, Claire. She's just running late as usual,' I said, trying to reassure her. 'She's going to walk through that door any second. I mean, can you imagine Brooke letting the two of us loose in Europe without her?'

Claire feigned a smile, anxiety written all over her face. She was such a worrywart, and as usual, I knew she was wasting her time fretting over something that was highly unlikely, especially today. 'Stop stressing over nothing, Claire,' we would tell her regularly. But that was our lovely Claire, like I said, a worrywart.

I knew Brooke would be here at any tick of the clock. This was the trip we'd all fantasised about for too long, the trip we'd all talk about for years to come – our European adventure. So yes, Brooke would definitely turn up today.

Claire was checking her watch for the umpteenth time when Brooke suddenly appeared as if she had all the time in the world. Richard had brought her. I smiled as I watched Brooke go through her usual apology routine with Claire. It wouldn't take long for Claire to forgive her. Brooke's charm was pure magic.

Richard edged his way over to me and discreetly passed me an envelope. 'Lucy, can you make sure Brooke gets this? But wait till she's on the plane before you give it to her,' he whispered.

'Sure, Richard, no problem. Is everything okay?'

'Yep, it's all good.' He smiled. I knew it was far from all good. Deep down, he hadn't wanted her to go. Six months was way too long for him to be without her. 'Why do you want to travel to Europe with the girls instead of with me?' he'd asked her when she first told him of our plan. She'd run wild in Europe with the girls, we determined, was the subtext.

They'd been seeing each other on and off – more off from Brooke's doing – for close to two years, and Richard was besotted with her. It wasn't like they lived together or anything, but he did ask her to marry him once, and she'd turned him down. She did love Richard in her own way, but the idea of becoming his wife and having to take on various household chores had never been at the top of her agenda. Richard was very good-looking, kind, and generous. He was also a successful architect and possessed all the credentials Brooke looked for in a man, but her free-spirited nature and relentless desire to travel had always prevented her from making any real commitment to him. Richard was twelve years older than Brooke, and he knew that she still had some wild oats to sow as evidenced by him each time they had their mini-break-ups. Regardless of what Richard knew in his heart of hearts, he loved her deeply. Today was always going to be a difficult day for Richard.

Brooke looked fabulous as usual, and her huge smile showed she'd already forgotten about leaving poor Richard. She was wearing a stylish black jacket over a black singlet and black capri pants. Her freshly streaked blond hair was shining above her like a halo. Her gorgeous brown eyes were sparkling, and her ruby red lipstick only served to emphasise that killer smile.

Both Brooke and Claire looked gorgeous. *Maybe I should've dressed up a bit more for the occasion*, I thought, but I'd always been a bit of a 'jeans and T-shirt' girl, especially when travelling. At least my own shoulder-length hair had just been redone with a load of blond streaks, which I thought looked nice. I was even wearing some make-up for the journey.

Claire was smiling now, so I knew it was safe to approach. Brooke and I hugged like we hadn't seen each other in years. 'Can you believe it, gorge? Today's the day. And before you ask,' she declared, unzipping her shoulder bag and presenting hard evidence, 'I have in my possession one liberating passport, one beautiful airline ticket to complete happiness, and all the money I need to get me to London via Europe.' The three of us laughed as we recalled the many hours spent agonising over what clothes, shoes, bags, jewellery, make-up, etc. we'd take with us, finally resolving that as long as we had our passports, tickets, and money, nothing else mattered. Whether it was a subtle message from above, however, it did cross my mind – fleetingly – that having to rely on a wing and a prayer might enter the equation at some stage of our journey.

The time had come to bid farewell to family and friends. It was a bittersweet moment as we hugged and kissed our loved ones goodbye, knowing we wouldn't see them again for six months. My sisters and I shed a few tears, but they were happy for me and insisted that I take care of myself and enjoy my time away. I knew I was going to miss them big time.

Claire's mum was giving her a final rundown of the do's and don'ts of travelling and told her to beware of anyone who looked suspicious. It was no wonder that Claire was a born worrier. She was hugging Claire like she'd never see her again, while Luke waited patiently to say his own goodbye, finally stepping in to kiss her sheepishly on the cheek.

Richard looked lost, and Brooke did her best to look sad as she kissed and hugged him one last time. Dear, sweet Richard.

We checked ourselves in at the departure desk and made our way towards the inner sanctum of Brisbane International Airport. 'Are we ready for this or what, girlfriends?' screamed Brooke. The three of us were hugging now, barely able to contain ourselves as our European adventure was finally happening. This was the day we had planned long and hard for.

We headed straight to the airport bar and ordered gin and tonics. 'To Europe', said Brooke, raising her glass.

'To Europe', echoed Claire and I. No sooner had we clinked our glasses in celebration than we heard the final call to Singapore being announced.

'What happened to the first call?' asked Brooke.

I knew what Claire was thinking. 'Let's do it then,' I said excitedly.

We quickly downed our drinks and left the bar with three of the biggest smiles known to mankind. Travellers alike were also merging in on our excitement, sharing the joy as we raced towards the departure gate and freedom. Europe was beckoning, and we were hot to trot. Already late, we decided that another couple of minutes wouldn't go amiss as we stopped to take some last-minute happy snaps against the backdrop of the huge Jumbo Jet, our winged transport to fun in the sun. We looked up in awe at the gigantic aircraft and couldn't help but observe several irritable faces glaring down onto the tarmac, watching us engage in our first exciting photo opportunity. Two flight attendants were at the bottom of the steps, frantically calling and waving at us to get a move on.

'It looks like we're the last to board,' said Claire, quickly zipping her camera back up in its case and throwing it into her handbag. Brooke and I followed suit.

'This is it, girls. This is the moment we've been waiting for!' yelled Brooke as the three of us ran excitedly towards the front of the plane. This was the beginning of our overseas adventure, and we were sick with excitement. It was 14 June 1988. D-Day was finally here.

CHAPTER TWO

WE ALL LOVED flying. Brooke and I had even applied to become trolley dollies once but failed miserably at the group interview. Everything had been going well, and we thought we were definitely in with a chance. We knew we looked the part, not to mention the many nights spent practising in front of the powder room mirror of our local nightclub demonstrating the safety equipment, much to the amusement and sometimes annoyance of legitimate lipstick users. Practice had, indeed, made perfect. Our arm and hand movements directing passengers to the forward and rear exit doors were faultless and our well-rehearsed smiles and emergency faces were committed to the care of all passengers.

During the group interview, we were split into teams and given several tasks and role-playing scenarios to act out so that the panel could observe how we all related to one another and how everyone handled various situations. When asked by one of the panel, however, to demonstrate airway, breathing, and circulation (ABC), the most basic first aid procedure, Brooke could only produce her famous smile and had looked to me for the answer. For once in her life, Brooke's beautiful show of pearly whites failed to impress as the panel, clearly unmoved by her best feature, immediately directed the question to me. *Oh no, please, God, get them to ask me something else,* I thought, my heart sinking rapidly as I tried desperately to remember the moves for ABC.

Two of the panel were already making notes on what looked like two application forms. *Surely that's got to be strike no.1 for both of us?* I thought despondently, citing a most inopportune time to lose one's memory. I looked at Brooke, whose once carefree face was now one of concern.

Well, I guess we had that coming as what self-respecting traveller would want Brooke and me in their corner during a life and death situation? I continued to myself.

'God, Brooke, my mind's gone completely blank,' I said under my breath.

'Mine too, Lucy. We shouldn't have had that last drink last night,' she replied. The two of us tried our hardest not to laugh out loud.

At the end of the gruelling session came question and answer time. Without a second thought, my hand was recklessly in the air. 'Are we allowed to date the flight attendants?' I asked gamely, trying to lighten the serious mood everyone seemed to be in. Well, let's face it, wasn't this job supposed to be about having some fun too? My sudden rise to infamy was evident as all heads turned to determine which one of us had boldly asked such a thing. Mutterings of 'what the?' and 'is she mad?' prompted me to question my question. I felt Brooke's elbow firmly in my side.

'Okay, so *maybe* I should've kept that one to myself,' I whispered, acknowledging my impetuousness. It seemed that I'd dared to ask the unthinkable, a question that could well have been on the minds and sealed lips of several of the applicants, yet I knew in a nanosecond that I was going to be the on-the-spot fall guy for putting myself out there with it.

Once the shock waves had desisted, an unwavering quiet descended on the room as everyone waited with interest for the panel's response. I bravely held the withering glares of the panel as their unforgiving eyes burnt holes through my once ardent body – a body that now felt like it was being turned to stone by the ancient Greek gorgons, three terrifying sisters in Greek mythology with serpent tails, scaly skin and venomous snakes for hair, which were now hissing at me disapprovingly. 'Well, certainly not *during* the flight,' came a somewhat harsh, stern reply. I couldn't help but hear some faint sniggers in the background. I was still wishing I'd never asked the question as the panel continued making notes on two application forms.

'Do you think they're still writing on our forms, Lucy?' Brooke whispered.

'I don't know. It's hard to tell,' I whispered back.

'What if they *are* our forms and it's all bad?' Brooke whispered again.

'Well, if that's the case, Brooke, they know nothing about hiring good, fun people,' I whispered back indignantly.

After twenty minutes of further questions from the floor – and no more from me, I hasten to add – the three probably mid to late forties all-female panel gathered up the fifty or so application forms and left the room for a final thirty-minute break before the group interview concluded. As soon as they closed the door behind them, bountiful sighs of relief could be heard from all candidates as they began analysing their own, *my*, and one another's performances. 'We really need to make it through to the next round, Lucy,' Brooke said categorically.

'I know, Brooke. The thing is we know we'd be great at this, so let's just hope they realise it too, despite a couple of setbacks,' I replied. My heart was heavy as I internalised those setbacks.

We sat there for what felt like an eternity, waiting for three people, who knew nothing about us, decide our future. Brooke and I were going over everything we had and hadn't said and done for the millionth time when the door opened, and the panel returned. We braced ourselves and watched in angst as they took to their chairs. The room was filled with anticipation and dreams as each and every one of us hoped and prayed for acceptance into the ether. Okay, so we made a couple of errors, but who doesn't during an interview? We tried to remain positive, deciding that we were still in the running for the jobs of our lifetime. The panel's expressionless faces remained unchanged as one of them announced that all candidates would be advised in the next week or so about who would be going through to the next round. They thanked everyone for coming and wished us all good luck.

'Oh god, this is going to be the most agonising time ever,' said Brooke despondently.

'I know, but let's stay hopeful, and it might be that you and I are just what they're looking for – flight attendants with some spunk,' I reasoned.

'I hope you're right, Lucy,' said Brooke.

'Of course, I am. I'd hire us, wouldn't you?' I added with optimism.

Less than a week had gone by, and the news we received hit us like a thunderbolt. The results were in, and we were out. This certainly wasn't one of our better days, and we were gobsmacked beyond belief. In all the time Brooke and I had known each other, we had discussed the whys and wherefores of a life in the sky, a career that would take us away from the corporate world of boredom, a career that would provide us with the excitement we desperately craved, a career that would allow us to experience different cultures and to meet people from all walks of life – not to mention the two of us being the friendliest and most fun-loving hosties ever to have walked, or should I say *flown*, the planet. Upon examining our failure to get through to the next round of interviews, we deduced that perhaps our kind of *fun-loving* wasn't exactly what the airline had in mind.

CHAPTER THREE

SO THERE WE were – Brooke, Claire, and I – happily ensconced in the middle section of the 747 Jumbo Jet, watching the crew I had wanted to date take us through the safety procedures. Brooke and I knew their every move. The good-looking flight attendant nearest to us was quite the comedian as he proceeded to make a slingshot from the oxygen mask, pointing it directly at us while placing the whistle from the life jacket in his ear. *So it was okay to have fun as a flight attendant, not to mention all my dreams possibly coming true on the Brisbane to Singapore sector,* I summated excitedly. We watched with envy as the cabin crew served meals and poured drinks, smiling and chatting to passengers. We also watched with envy as everyone admired them moving gracefully through the cabin.

Brooke looked at me with renewed enthusiasm. 'There's nothing to stop us from applying again, Lucy,' she declared. 'We can do this job with our eyes closed.'

'We certainly can, Brooke, not to mention what we can do with our eyes open,' I quipped. We continued checking out the good-looking flight attendant, at the same time making mental notes to contact the airline again the moment we returned from Europe.

After lunch and a few gin and tonics later, it was nail extension time for Brooke. Her own nails were short from the endless typing of legal documents in her boring office job, and as I'd mastered the art of gluing tips onto my own nails, she'd enlisted me as her personal manicurist. Without further ado, she disappeared into her bag of tricks, emerging with a packet of plastic nails, a pair of scissors, emery boards, nail glue, tissues, and a selection of polish, our tray tables suddenly transformed into an in-flight nail bar. I spent the next hour sizing, cutting, filing, shaping, gluing, and buffing, with a final round of filing, gluing, and buffing until my client was happy. I must say that despite the effects of lunchtime alcohol and occasional turbulence, I did a pretty good job. A French polish completed the task, and as soon as her nails were dry, I handed her the envelope from Richard.

'What's this?' she asked, surprised.

'Richard gave it to me at the airport for you and said you had to open it on the plane,' I replied.

'Maybe it's a goodbye Johnny letter,' she said jokingly.

'Or it could be a love letter,' said Claire, always the romantic.

'Well, there's only one way to find out,' I added hastily.

Brooke ripped it open. Five-hundred-dollars cold, hard cash was in the envelope. Brooke's face was an absolute picture, like she'd just hit the biggest jackpot prize ever. We all knew how much Richard loved Brooke and that he'd wanted her to have a good time, even though she'd chosen Claire and me over him. God bless Richard. If ever there was a man who loved a woman, it was Richard who loved Brooke. He worshipped the ground she walked on and would do absolutely anything for her, even though he knew that she'd undoubtedly get up to no good while she was away. I guess Richard was just waiting for the day when Brooke would leave her itinerant ways with the girls behind her and say yes, finally, to settling down and becoming his wife.

'Ah god, isn't he gorgeous!' exclaimed Brooke, an adjective she used to describe everyone she knew – and some she'd only just met. 'The first round of drinks when we get to the Greek islands is on Richard.' We ordered more gin and tonics and raised our glasses in his honour.

Our good-looking flight attendant approached us. 'You can come upstairs now, girls,' he said, ushering us to the spiral staircase. Our earlier request to visit the flight deck had been granted, and so the three of us spent the next two hours with the captain and his crew, chatting about everything from the exotic places they'd visited to possible UFO sightings. The exotic places sounded, well, exotic; and comments made by the captain and the first officer that inexplicable objects had, in fact, been sighted by them left us in no doubt that UFOs actually did exist.

Brooke and I were beside ourselves with excitement, Claire not so much, in the hope that we might actually see a flying saucer. They chatted to us about our plans for Europe and were impressed that we'd taken six months off work to go travelling. We tried their caps on for size, and the captain took our photo for posterity. The handsome purser arrived. 'Is everything okay up here?' he asked.

'Absolutely. We are having the most amazing time. Thank you,' I replied, staring into his gorgeous face.

'Good.' He smiled. 'Just let me know if there's anything I can get you.'

Wow, you can get me you, I thought, holding his charismatic gaze. He stayed for a while, and I could feel my heart pulsating as he stood close to me in the confined space. I breathed in the seductive fragrance of his cologne, or was it just his raw magnetism that was playing havoc with my senses? Whatever it was, I thought I was going to pass out from it when Claire spotted another plane flying below us, jolting me out of my hot flush.

'Isn't that plane flying a bit too close?' she asked the captain with concern.

'No, they're good. They're on a different flight path to ours, so no need to worry. It's a big sky. We've all got plenty of room,' he replied calmly.

Claire let out a sigh of relief, prompting the rest of us to laugh. Claire laughed too, albeit a nervous one. God bless Claire.

The three of us relished the time spent with these highly experienced pilots in the attic of this huge Jumbo Jet, leaving us feeling thrilled and privileged. In fact, the whole flight deck experience couldn't have been a more amazing start to our holiday. But wait, there's more. The captain invited us to join them for dinner and drinks at their hotel that evening. What were we like? Three lustful young girls bound for Europe and already scoring dates from gorgeous men in uniform, and the plane hadn't even landed yet. At 33,000 feet, perhaps the Mile High Club had set its sights on us after all. *Suck this up, ladies,* was my telepathic message back to the interview panel.

CHAPTER FOUR

A T CHANGI AIRPORT and sadly missing out on dinner and drinks with the captain and his crew, Brooke and Claire boarded a flight to Athens. We'd all agreed when mapping out our itinerary that, because I'd never been to Singapore, I'd take the opportunity to stop over for a night and a day to check it out. I would then catch a flight to London, collect three other girlfriends who were due for a two-week vacation, and fly to the island of Rhodes in Greece. A taxi would be taken to the village of Lindos, where we would meet up with Brooke and Claire for celebratory cocktails at the Sparkle Bar on 20 June on the stroke of midnight. On this date and by this time, Brooke and Claire would have arrived in Lindos, having ferried their way down from Athens. Our drinks rendezvous had been planned with military precision. The three of us would then wind our way through Europe up to the United Kingdom, where Brooke and I would find secretarial work to make enough money to buy our tickets home, and Claire would fly directly to Norway to visit her sister, Susan, and family.

We said our goodbyes, and it felt weird that our threesome was splitting up so soon. 'Have the best time in Athens and see you in Lindos,' I said, hugging both of them.

'Watch yourself with those airline charmers. You don't know them,' came Claire's concerned reply.

'Just have fun, baby,' ordered an enthused Brooke, giving me that *go for it* wink.

With mixed feelings, I watched them walk away until they were almost out of sight. They turned for one more goodbye wave. 'I miss you already!' I called out after them, but they didn't hear me. So there I was, in the blink of an eye, alone in Singapore, wondering if I'd made the right decision to stay in this unfamiliar place by myself; after all, wasn't this trip supposed to be about the three of us travelling together? I was glad I had the company of the captain and his crew to look forward to. I was also more than looking forward to seeing the handsome purser again.

I caught a taxi to my hotel, which coincidentally was the same hotel the airline crew were staying at. I was relieved that I didn't have far to travel for dinner, relieved too that I didn't have far to travel after dinner should too much alcohol become an issue. After I checked in, a nice young porter carried my precious suitcase and accompanied me to the tenth floor. My room was really lovely, and I had the most spectacular view. I smiled. I'd made it to Singapore, the first leg of a long and exciting journey ahead. Whether it was from sheer excitement or jet lag, I could feel my eyes starting to close.

I phoned reception for a wake-up call, lay down on top of the bed, and drifted off into tranquillity. I'd been asleep for two hours when the phone rang. 'Wake-up call for you, ma'am,' the nice female Singaporean voice said.

I had the longest shower and felt all faculties slowly returning to normal. I dried my hair, put on some make-up, sprayed my entire body with duty-free perfume, slipped on my favourite little black dress, and stepped into my sparkly black stilettos. I poured myself a drink from the minibar and decided I was going to have a great evening. I toasted the girls and ventured downstairs to meet the guys.

Lucky me, I spent the evening dining and drinking Martinis with the captain, the first officer, the gorgeous purser, and the slingshot flight attendant. I couldn't help wishing the other two angels were with me, but what the heck, the odds were all in my favour – maybe I didn't miss the girls that much after all. The food was delicious. 'I'm a vegetarian and don't eat anything with a face or a bum,' I'd told them, and so they took great care in making sure my meal was animal-free. My first night in Singapore, and I was having the best time. The purser had also given me a bottle of gin before I left the plane, and I couldn't wipe the smile off my face. The guys were great fun, and we ate, drank, chatted, and laughed the hours away.

The captain was a distinguished-looking older man. He was very knowledgeable about the world and had a great sense of humour. His gold wedding ring was very noticeable. 'You must miss your family when you're away all the time?' I questioned.

'Sure, I do,' he said matter-of-factly. 'But the kids are all grown up now, and my wife still works for the airline, which means she flies a lot too. And after thirty odd years of travelling, we're kind of used to not seeing each other all the time.'

'But don't you get tempted when you're away? You know,' I jokingly inquired.

'No, I don't,' he declared. 'And even if I did, just look at these good-looking single young guys I have to travel with. I don't stand a chance with them around.' He laughed.

One of those good-looking single young guys was, of course, the purser, who'd been paying me a fair amount of attention both on the flight deck and throughout the evening. He was around 183 cm, handsome, charming, and seriously sexy. I'd say he would've been around 30 years old. His eyes were brown, almost the same colour as his neatly cut hair. His mouth was extremely sensual, and I could only imagine what it would feel like to kiss it with mine. He was intelligent, made interesting conversation, and just oozed with confidence.

I was attracted to him from the moment we met, so much so that throughout the entire evening – and not wanting the whole world to witness my out-of-control desire towards him – I made several pathetic attempts to not breathe heavily, not make my pupils dilate, and not go all hearts and flowers every time he looked at me, making little to no progress whatsoever. It didn't help either that he sat next to me at the table, often putting his arm around my shoulder and pulling me in close to him, making sure I was enjoying myself and had everything I needed. I think it was pretty obvious that I failed miserably at trying to hide such clear-cut infatuation.

The first officer was more the strong, silent type. He looked in his mid to late forties and had a warm, friendly face, salt-and-pepper hair, and a good physique. He was very polite and laughed at everyone's jokes. He was genuinely interested in everything everyone said and was obviously well respected by the crew. He revisited our trip. 'I think it's wonderful that you've all taken six months off work to travel. I'm sure a lot of girls your age wouldn't dream of quitting their jobs to embark on such a venture,' he commented.

'Well, it's something all three of us have wanted to do for a while now. And as we're all fully qualified secretaries, I'm sure we'll have no problem getting work when we get back,' I replied.

'Good for you.' He smiled.

'You must love your job, flying Jumbo Jets around the world?' I asked.

'Yes, most definitely', he replied. 'For as long as I can remember, I've been fascinated with planes. We lived near an airport when I was a young lad, and I'd watch them coming in to land and take off.' He smiled. 'Flying planes was the only thing I ever wanted to do.'

'Well, I think you all do an amazing job,' I told him in no uncertain terms.

'I certainly hope so, seeing as it's not the sort of job that allows for mistakes,' he said resolutely. We carried on chatting, and he was interested to hear that I'd worked as a junior typist at Heathrow Airport when I was 15 during the school holidays.

'Barry, my brother-in-law, worked in customs and excise and organised a job for me. Every spare second I had, I'd stand outside, watching the planes coming in to land and take off, a bit like you actually,' I told him, also reminiscing with a smile.

'Barry even presented me with a gold-painted model of a VC10 on a stand, which I treasured and kept on my dressing table for years,' I concluded with pride. He was pleased that I shared his love for planes, and we had a nice connection.

The slingshot flight attendant? Well, apart from obviously possessing an even-tempered, confident, and caring persona – oh, and I must add multitasker to the list – I think he was also about having as much fun as he could muster. He was blond and definitely good-looking and had a body to die for. He was a great conversationalist and extremely funny. He had so many stories to tell and kept us amused with the comical situations he faced daily, often getting up and demonstrating various scenarios. In fact, I don't think I ever saw him without a smile on his face throughout the entire evening, not to mention how much fun he was on the flight. He talked about some of the girls he'd dated and even some of the boys he'd been out with, finally realising that he was definitely gay.

'You do realise that being so gorgeous *and* gay is a tragedy as far as the female race is concerned,' I remarked.

He welcomed my thinking and without missing a beat said, 'Darling, I would have *turned* just for you had you been continuing your flight up to London with us.' Of course, he made us all laugh with his tongue-in-cheek statement, pardon the pun. He did mention that the present love of his life was also a flight attendant.

Well, blow me, I thought – and pardon the second pun in as many sentences – *how did he manage to get through his group interview as I'm sure he couldn't have resisted asking the panel about dating the crew?*

As much as I was having the most wonderful time, it was getting late. I was thanking everyone for their wonderful company and generosity when, and not entirely to my surprise, the purser stood up. 'Allow me to escort you to your room,' he announced.

'See what I mean?' the captain confirmed. 'How can I compete with that?'

'Oh, I reckon you could still give these guys a run for their money,' I responded with sincerity, smiling at the handsome captain. He was obviously happy with my response.

The purser was still waiting for my answer, and so, it seemed, by the look on their faces, were the rest of my dinner companions. 'Gosh, no, you really don't need to, but thank you anyway. It's very kind of you to offer, but I'll be fine. I really don't have far to go,' I replied, trying to be polite yet desperately wanting him not to take no for an answer.

'It's no problem,' he insisted.

Thank you, God. I smiled.

'Plus, you never know who you might find lurking around the elevators,' he joked.

'In fact, only recently, I heard a rumour that a middle-aged man with grey hair wearing an airline uniform was loitering in that very area on the lookout for pretty young girls like you,' he added, nodding towards the captain. Everyone laughed as the captain pleaded his innocence to the purser's facetious accusation.

I went along with the joke. 'Well, in that case, I would be honoured to have such a strong, brave escort. Thank you,' I replied.

'Some guys have all the luck,' the captain remarked, winking at me. I was relieved the purser hadn't taken my refusal as gospel.

We arrived at my door and stood outside for a few minutes, chatting. The attraction was clearly mutual, and I naturally thought about inviting him in for coffee, but before I could ask, he leaned in to kiss me. It was soft and sensual at first, just as I imagined it would be. I could feel his body pressed hard up against mine as his kisses became more urgent. I was kissing him back, lost in the passion with this gorgeous man. Multiple shivers were invading my spine, and after a pash like that, surely he deserved at least one coffee? But we all know that inviting someone in for coffee doesn't *really* mean inviting them in for just coffee, does it? Plus, it's just the most banal *come fuck me* line ever. Coffee or no coffee, it was pretty obvious he wanted to come in. *Okay, so what if this handsome, sexy guy wants to seduce me? I totally fancy him, so just invite him in. You know you want to*, I told myself, at the same time asking myself why I was hesitating.

So there I was, locked in the purser's masculine embrace, imagining how incredible it would be to have hot sex with this gorgeous guy when, totally out of the blue, I had a supersonic flashback. In my mind's eye and in full-blown 3D colour, I'd transported myself back in time to the group interview for the airline. I could see the blood draining rapidly from the moral and righteous faces of the panel, their eyes narrowing in abhorrence, when I'd asked about dating the crew. I watched in sheer terror as their condemnation and loathing towards me evolved faster than the speed of light. Their distorted, evil faces danced in and around me as the droning sounds of disapproval from my fellow candidates reverberated inside my head. In their virtuous minds, I was the antithesis of everything good and honourable. Without even a fair trial, I'd been found guilty of premeditated sin, duly sentenced to a life on solid ground.

L. A. FLORRIE

I pulled away from him, my heart racing. 'Are you okay? You look like you've seen a ghost,' he asked, concerned.

'No. I mean, yes, I'm fine, thank you. I'm just feeling a little dizzy from all those Martinis. I'm sorry, but do you mind if I don't invite you in? I think I may have had one too many, and I'll probably fall asleep on you anyway,' I heard myself telling him.

What are you doing, you crazy woman? This man is hot! screamed my inner self.

He looked disappointed but was very much the gentleman. 'Of course, no problem at all,' he said. 'You have a good sleep, and if you're free for lunch tomorrow, how about I take you to a great little vegetarian restaurant I know?'

'That would be lovely,' I replied, my body and soul now wanting to drag him into my room and rip his clothes off, the nightmarish visions of the interview panel dematerialising as quickly as they came.

'Great. I'll need to be back here at 3 p.m. to leave for my next flight, so how about I come up at midday?' I could only nod. He kissed me again and left.

I stumbled into my room like an infirm person and leaned up against the door for support, my lips and entire body still tingling from the intensity of his full-on pash. My heart was pumping blood at an alarming rate. *What is wrong with you? Are you completely insane?* I asked my incompetent brain. I looked over at the beautifully made-up double bed, and all I could see were lascivious images of what would've no doubt transpired had I invited him in. I'd failed to take advantage of a rare opportunity to have a night of wonderful impromptu sex with a man most girls would lay down and die for, yet despite my woeful, not to mention my most regrettable refusal of entry decision to date, he'd still invited me out to lunch. I didn't even know this man, and regardless of Claire's warning, it was obvious his moral compass was pointing in the right direction, and she would've been pleased with his integrity. I, on the other hand, was not so pleased with my somewhat confused, whatever compass and would forever look back with disappointment on one of the most abysmal decisions I'd ever made.

I wandered over to the window and gazed out across the city skyline, taking in the twinkling lights of Singapore, my despondent reflection staring back at me. 'You're an idiot' were the last words I said to myself that night.

CHAPTER FIVE

I SLEPT IN THE next morning till around eight thirty and arrived downstairs for breakfast in the restaurant half an hour later. I didn't see him or the crew and assumed that they must have been at an earlier sitting. After a leisurely first meal of the day, nibbling on fresh fruit, tea, and toast, I had two hours to kill before lunch – a lunch that may or may not still be on the cards.

I wandered over to the reception area and sat there for a while, people watching. I wrote some postcards back to Oz, letting everyone know that I was still alive, even though it had only been a day and a half. I flicked through some magazines and took a stroll around the hotel, and before I knew it, it was almost time. I took the elevator back up to my room and felt excited at the prospect of seeing him again. While I was deciding what to wear, the thought crossed my mind again that he could be a no-show. After all, he certainly didn't owe me anything and was well within his rights to stand me up.

I stopped what I was doing and sat down on the bed. I told myself that it didn't matter if he didn't show up, that I'd planned all along to stay in Singapore alone and have a look around, so that was what I would still do. I continued getting ready, and as there was no forecast for rain, only sunshine and humidity, I decided to wear my favourite short light blue cotton shift dress that had small white flowers printed on it and my white walking pumps. I put on some mascara and some neutral-coloured lipstick and pulled my hair up into a ponytail.

At precisely twelve o'clock, there was a knock on my door. It was him. *Thank you, God, again.*

He was casually yet smartly dressed in a white linen shirt and dark grey linen shorts and looked hotter than ever. 'Hi, are you ready for a taste sensation?' he asked.

I smiled, delighted that he'd turned up. 'Most certainly', I replied. 'Where are we going?'

'You'll find out soon enough.' He laughed. 'If you're ready, we should go. I have a cab waiting downstairs.'

Maybe the cab can wait, I debated with myself, again critiquing last night's doomed coffee invitation, but he'd already pressed for the elevator, and the moment was gone.

Let this be a lesson to you, I told myself. *He who hesitates is well and truly lost.*

As the weatherman had predicted on the television that morning, it was a hot and humid day as we drove along the lush, tropical streets. With its backdrop of skyscrapers, the city was busy with people on their way to lunch, shoppers by the droves, and a million tourists with cameras around their necks. We passed the famous Raffles Hotel, one of Singapore's most charming colonial landmarks. Named after Sir Stamford Raffles, the founder of modern Singapore in 1819, this luxurious hotel stood proud in the heart of the city. We passed the beautiful shops and restaurants along Orchard Road, and it wasn't difficult to feel the romance and excitement of this enchanting island.

I'm completely insane for not inviting him in last night, I told myself for the hundredth time, glancing at him as he sat close to me in the taxi. *I just know I'm going to regret this when I'm 90. If only he wasn't leaving this afternoon.* The scent of his cologne was again intoxicating, and I had wild visions of being completely ravished by him had he been able to stay one more night.

He looked at me and smiled his perfect smile. 'How's your head? Not too hung-over from all those Martinis, I hope?' he inquired with concern.

'No, I feel great actually,' I replied, looking deep into his eyes. 'I think I just needed a good night's sleep.'

Oh god, what I really needed was a hot night with you, I bleated to myself.

He was even better looking today than last night, and I found myself staring at him. He knew I was ogling. 'Have you ever thought of becoming a model?' I blurted out, substantiating my interest.

'Me? No way.' He laughed 'Why do you ask?'

OMG, you are so incredibly hot. Isn't it obvious? I thought.

'Well, it's just that you're kind of not bad looking, and you've got a really cute smile,' I said matter-of-factly.

'And your body isn't too bad either,' I joked, quickly scanning his physique from where I was sitting.

'Well, if you think so, maybe I should give it some serious thought but only if you consider becoming my agent,' he joked back. 'And of course, you can take 10 per cent.'

I contemplated his offer. 'Well, I'd only ever consider becoming your personal manager, which by the way means I take *20 per cent*. Plus, I'd have to travel everywhere with you just to keep you on the straight and narrow,' I negotiated.

'Done', he said, holding out his hand. As we shook on the deal, he pulled me in close and kissed me.

If only Galileo had invented a way of turning back the clock, I thought as he sent tingling sensations all through my body once more.

CHAPTER SIX

T HE STREETS SUDDENLY became narrower, and we found ourselves in a quaint old shanty-cum-Chinatown, the cafes and shopfronts very ordinary in comparison to fashionable Orchard Road. There were vendors and restaurant staff on breaks, sitting on the pavement, chatting and waving to one another. The atmosphere was chaotic, with motorbikes tooting and cars honking, and the air was thick from the collision of smoke streaming out of several kitchen windows.

The taxi driver announced our arrival. We walked down half a dozen narrow wrought-iron steps to the little vegetarian cafe which seated about fifty. It was quite dimly lit, save for the daylight shimmering through the four small square windows above at street level. There were two ceiling fans. The tables were covered with red-and-white check plastic tablecloths, and the wooden chairs reminded me of the ones we used to sit on back at high school. Every table was occupied, except for a prearranged table for two. He escorted me to our table and pulled out my chair for me. 'Mademoiselle, your table awaits,' he said in a sexy authentic French accent.

'Merci, Monsieur,' I replied back in mine. I smiled and held his gaze as he sat down opposite me.

My imagination went into overdrive again as I visualised him dragging me onto the table, ripping my clothes off in the process, his unrelenting force holding me down as he proceeded to make wild, reckless love to me. My body was at his disposal, his strong physique playing no part in forgiveness. His untamed technique was invigorating as he continued to thrust himself deep inside me, bringing me to heights I'd conceptualised he could, his rapacious mouth vehemently exploring mine. Unrestrained with an insatiable hunger for flesh, he was a man possessed, and I was the ultimate sacrifice. I died a million beautiful deaths.

'How's your appetite?' he asked.

My imaginary glorious fate was still spread across the table. 'I'm sorry, what did you say?' came my breathless response.

'How's your appetite?' he repeated.

'Good, I'm feeling quite ravenous actually,' I replied, still quite breathless and again staring at him with thoughts of *If only you knew how ravenous I really am and for what.*

'Are you okay?' he enquired. 'Your throat sounds kind of dry. Would you like some water?'

'Yes, thank you. Some water would be great. It's actually quite warm and humid in here, so water would be really good,' I replied, fanning myself with the bamboo table mat, authenticating my sudden state of hotness. My immoral thoughts were out of control, and as there was no window of opportunity left between now and his next flight to impart just how sexually attracted to him I was, I decided to centralise my mind on the matter at hand – food.

My rational appraisal of the situation couldn't have been more perfectly timed as it was met with the aroma of rice and spices gently wafting from the kitchen. 'Mmm, smells delicious,' I said with normal voice after sipping some water.

'Wait till you taste it,' he said without a hint of suspicion of my maniacal state.

We hadn't been seated there for long when a skinny little man who looked at least 120 years old arrived at our table, carrying a huge pan of rice. One of the waitresses brought two banana leaves to the table, and a portion of rice was placed on each leaf. The ancient rice man went back to the kitchen and returned with an amazing selection of local vegetables, tofu, and sauces. Apart from the traditional chopsticks on offer, cutlery didn't seem to be an option. 'I don't use chopsticks when I eat here,' my purser advised. He nodded discreetly at the tables around us.

I looked with equal discretion to see that the locals ate with their fingers. 'Well, when in Rome, as my dear old dad used to say,' I whispered.

I watched him closely as he ate without the aid of utensils. I was practically sliding off my seat as he provocatively deposited sauce-drenched fingers into his mouth, slowly licking each one of them dry. I was beginning to feel hot again, and breathlessness was once more becoming an issue. *Please send help immediately*, I implored my friend, the universe, as I sat within tangible reach of my seductive lunch date. *If divine intervention doesn't take place soon, I just know I'm going to embarrass myself big time.*

As I looked away to focus my mind on something less symbolic, my debauched thoughts were suddenly quashed by the waitress. 'How is everything, ma'am?' she inquired in perfect English.

'Oh, hi, yes, really good, thank you, very tasty,' I replied.

'Are you here in Singapore for business or holiday?' she asked.

'No, just a stopover unfortunately. I arrived yesterday, and I'm leaving tonight, so not very long at all, I'm afraid.'

'I hope maybe when you come back, you will stay for longer,' she invited.

'Oh, yes, most definitely. Your island is very beautiful, so I will definitely stay longer next time.' I smiled.

'And may I ask, sir, how is your lunch?'

'Absolutely delicious as always, thank you.' He smiled. The waitress looked at me with knowing eyes.

'I'm glad everything is good,' she said and walked away.

Wow, the cosmos is on form today, I thought as I sent my gratitude skywards.

My temperature was falling and my blood pressure no longer cause for concern. 'Could you tell me where the bathroom is?' I asked.

'Sure, it's the second door on the right, just past the kitchen,' he replied.

'Thanks, back soon.' I made it to the bathroom without incident, where I took some slow, deep breaths, together with a good hard look at myself in the mirror.

What is wrong with you? I asked myself. *You had your chance last night, and you blew it, so get over yourself.* After a good talking-to and a reality check, I splashed my face with cold water as extra assurance. No longer flushed, I returned to the table and remained composed as we chatted over a fried banana dessert and green tea. I was glad my drop-dead handsome escort had brought me to this sweet little place.

'How long have you been with the airline?' I asked, my mind now off the obvious.

'Ten years almost to the day,' he replied. 'I've got the best job in the world, flying around the globe, experiencing different cultures, and meeting all sorts of people, not to mention lovely girls like you.' It was obvious he wasn't ready to settle down and have kids, and from what he intimated, it was easy to presume that he'd broken more than a few hearts along the way.

'So I guess you have a girlfriend waiting for you in every port,' I teased.

'Well, not *every* port', he teased back.

Mmm, with a face and body like yours, I bet you do, I thought to myself.

'My friend and I tried to get into an airline once back in Oz,' I told him. 'But they knocked us back. I think they thought we were just out for fun and free plane rides around the world, which was 95 per cent true.' I laughed.

He looked at me with his gorgeous brown eyes and took my hand. 'Well, if it's any consolation, I think you'd make an amazing air hostess. You're fun, good with people. You seem caring and composed. In fact, I think you've got everything going for you. I also think you'd be completely level-headed in an emergency situation,' he summarised.

As long as you weren't part of the emergency, I thought.

'Why, thank you very much, kind sir,' I replied in my best deep South American accent. 'Maybe I'll apply for a job with your airline next time.'

Our conversation was light and fun; in fact, the whole afternoon had been fun, not to mention a little hot under the collar once or twice. We didn't get into the deep and meaningful; there wasn't enough time for that. After our delicious meal, we caught a cab back to the hotel. It was time for my purser to leave for the airport and his next flight. 'Take care of yourself and enjoy Europe,' he said. 'And don't be too hard on all those boys you're going to meet and fall in love with.'

I looked into his big brown eyes. 'Thanks for everything, and don't *you* be too hard on all those girls *you're* going to keep on meeting and falling in love with either,' I replied. A big hug and another full-on pash, and he was gone. Again, I was left alone to deal with serious tingling sensations as I watched him walk out of my life. If only I'd been on his plane up to London and not a later one. We didn't exchange phone numbers, and it was pretty obvious that we'd never see each other again.

I felt somewhat sad saying goodbye to him and again questioned myself why I hadn't invited him in the night before; after all, wasn't a tall dark handsome man in uniform every girl's dream? Temporary insanity came to mind, and I told myself that this condition would pass quickly and not attach itself to me for the next six months. And it was right there and then, at that defining moment in Singapore, I decided nothing was going to stop me from letting go and taking a walk on the wild side. *From now on, this journey is going to be all about livin' and lovin'*, I vowed to myself.

I had the rest of the afternoon free, so I jumped on a tour bus that took in some of the tourist spots, concluding in a visit to the colourful Tiger Balm Garden, now Haw Par Villa, which contained hundreds of statues depicting ancient Chinese folklore and Confucianism. The colourful gardens were built by the Aw family to promote their Tiger Balm product, a renowned ointment for easing aches and pains.

As we approached the impressive Paifang, a large crowd of local vendors were there, milling around with huge cobras draped around their necks, all of them calling out to us to have our photos taken with their snakes. I must have been mad (*permanent* insanity was now looking more likely), but the snake owner kept telling me, 'Charlie no bite, Charlie good, Charlie okay, Miss.'

'Ah well,' I replied, 'if Charlie no bite . . .'

He put Charlie around my neck, and I gave my camera to the nice lady I'd sat next to on the tour bus to take a photo. As she was trying to work out which button to push, Charlie started making his way down from my shoulders, slowly wrapping his huge, long, and extremely heavy body around my waist. I was trying to stay calm, not wanting Charlie to sense my fear, but I could feel the panic slowly beginning to set in. My amateur photographer was still working out which button to push, finally calling out from a safe distance to show me if she had her finger on the right button. 'Yes, yes, that's the one. Please hurry and take the photo!' I wailed in desperation.

She asked me to say cheese as she very slowly started counting, 'one, two, three.'

'Just hurry up, will you?' I said under my breath, at the same time catching a glimpse of tomorrow's world headlines, DERANGED AUSTRALIAN TOURIST SQUEEZED TO DEATH BY CHARLIE THE COBRA IN SINGAPORE'S FAVOURITE FAMILY FUN PARK.

I managed to force a smile when she told me she had to take it again as the button hadn't worked. *Oh for crying out loud, just take the goddam photo!* The camera finally clicked, and Charlie's owner gently unwrapped him from around me. Everyone on the bus thought I was the bravest thing out, and so Charlie and I became the topic of conversation for the rest of the afternoon.

The tour bus took us back alongside the Singapore River, passing colonial-style buildings, Hindu temples, and churches in beautifully manicured tree-lined streets. If only I'd planned to spend more time in this gorgeous place. We arrived at the hotel and said our goodbyes to one another as we all went our separate ways. What an unforgettable time, albeit short, in beautiful Singapore.

I went up to my room to collect the rest of my belongings and took one last look at where I could have had the night of my life. It was time for me to board my flight to London.

CHAPTER SEVEN

I COULDN'T HELP WONDERING what Brooke and Claire were up to. Had they gotten to Athens in one piece? What was Athens like? What was the weather like in Athens? Had they found Greek lovers yet? Were they having fun without me?

I found my window seat on the plane and settled in for the long haul ahead. I felt like the luckiest girl in the world as I embarked on the second leg of my prodigious journey, barely able to breathe from excitement as the plane pushed back and commenced taxiing. I stared out into the vast unknown and contemplated the wild adventures that lay ahead, the sudden roar of the engines amplifying my fantasies as the plane surged down the runway, gathering speed by the millisecond.

As I was stolen away into the night sky, I thought I was going to burst from sheer ecstasy. I looked down onto the beautifully lit city of Singapore until it disappeared from view, smiling as thoughts of my purser prevailed. Still ascending at a million miles an hour, the upper stratosphere remained pitch-black as I searched in vain for the bright lights of a UFO. I leaned back into my seat and started to reminisce, slowly putting together the pieces of fate's jigsaw that had brought me to where I was at that moment.

CHAPTER EIGHT

I MET BROOKE AND Claire on the Gold Coast in Australia, where we all lived and worked as secretaries. Brooke and I both worked in law firms, and Claire worked in a real estate office. I knew Brooke's boss intimately, but that was another story. After he employed Brooke, he rang me straight away. 'You just *have* to meet my new secretary ASAP,' he announced with his trademark enthusiasm. I was glad I was sitting down as I knew he was going to go on and on about her. 'Anyway, she's just arrived back in Oz after spending a year living in your home town. It's where her mum was raised, so she flew over there to meet her long-lost relatives, picking up some temp work at the same time.'

Frankie was big into star signs and told me that when he interviewed Brooke, he noticed that her birthday was five days after mine, eagerly telling her that he once had a torrid love affair with a Gemini. 'Really, you told her that? In her interview?' I winced. Seriously, Frankie couldn't help himself sometimes.

'Look, I know you won't mind, but I just know you two will get on really well, so I've taken the liberty of arranging a luncheon for you both.' Always one for surprises, it was typical of him to organise such a thing. He kept telling me how alike Brooke and I were and that we'd have much in common, seeing as I'd emigrated from Liverpool to Oz only two years earlier; but more importantly, as far as Frankie was concerned, we were both born under the star sign of Gemini. Boy, did he hit the jackpot with our pairing.

Our first lunch together saw Brooke and me wearing exactly the same red and white outfits, right down to matching jewellery, bags, and shoes. Laughing hysterically, we couldn't get inside the cafe fast enough before anyone we knew saw us. We chatted like we'd known each other for a hundred years, almost taking the words out of each other's mouths. We both loved meeting people, both loved having a good time, both loved travelling, both worked in law firms – both not so keen on working in law firms – both worked in Liverpool, both now worked on the Gold Coast, both did this, both didn't do that. And that was the way it would be from that day on. Brooke and I were destined to meet. We were soul sisters, twins, best friends. We still are to this day.

Brooke was 173 cm and had the classic fuller figure. She was blond, vivacious, and gorgeous, and her personality was second to none. Her laugh was exuberant and infectious, and she lived each day like there was no tomorrow. Everyone – and I mean *everyone* – she came into contact with loved her, especially me. Brooke's undying love and passion for life rubbed off on everyone she met. She could hold an audience in the palms of both hands, telling story after story, until the cows came home. It didn't matter what yarn she told, and believe me, she told hundreds; she could turn it into the most intriguing and absorbing tale ever, keeping everyone on the edge of their seats for hours. Brooke could sell sand to the Arabs by the truckload and as white skinned and fair haired as she was, I watched her on many occasions convince countless people that she was a native from Botswana. Needless to say, they believed her.

Brooke and I laughed till our faces hurt, and our friendship couldn't have been more perfect. She hated routine and, like me, found herself working nine to five in a law firm out of necessity for money. We talked about breaking free from the confines of office humdrum and travelling to Europe together for six months, a plan that would provide us with the excitement and stimulation we so desperately craved, a plan that would give us hope for the future.

Claire and I met through Brooke on one of our many nights out, and I found her to be really sweet and easy to talk to. Claire was born under the sign of Capricorn, and although she could be a little reserved at times and mostly played her cards to her chest, she still loved being around people and having a good time. She was intelligent, pragmatic, and down-to-earth. She saw only the logical and was the sort of person who always planned for that rainy day. She was punctual and kind and didn't like to let people down. She cared about people and was loyal.

L. A. FLORRIE

She talked about getting married one day to a wonderful man, having children, and living her happily ever after. Claire had the warmest smile, and we knew that, one day, she would make the perfect wife for that special someone. She was a little shorter than Brooke, also had the fuller figure, and was all woman. It was good having Claire around as, even though she tended to worry more than most, a trait Brooke and I believed she inherited from her mother, she was the stable one, the one who never made rash decisions, the one who tried to keep us grounded, the sane one.

As soon as Claire heard about our plan for Europe, she asked if she could join us. 'Absolutely', replied Brooke and I keenly, our synchronicity in top form. The three of us talked non-stop about travelling overseas together. We made a point of meeting three times a week to discuss which countries we wanted to visit, how long we wanted to stay in each, which country we would start in, and where we would end up. We would sit on the floor in my unit, eating takeaway pizza and drinking wine, with the map of Europe spread out on the carpet. We sourced brochures from travel agents of the places we were interested in visiting and chatted at length about how much money we thought we'd need for six months. Needless to say, Claire always brought her calculator with her. We didn't see the need to book our holiday through a travel agent and couldn't foresee any obstacles with organising the holiday ourselves. All we needed to do was to book flights heading towards the northern hemisphere with a fair bit of our travelling in between, to be tackled by road, rail, and sea. It all seemed pretty straightforward and idiot-proof. Luckily, we were all on the same page, and the three of us worked well as the travel dream team to pull off the holiday of our lifetime.

It was only a matter of months before our European trip became a reality. Claire, also the shrewd one, had saved an impressive amount of money. Brooke and I, on the other hand, always having possessed an insatiable desire to go out clubbing seven nights a week invariably meant that our holiday fund paled in comparison and the reason why we'd only been able to afford one-way tickets. If only we'd been Capricorns instead of Geminis, our European trip would have turned out completely differently. But then perhaps I wouldn't have been writing this book.

CHAPTER NINE

AFTER A LONG flight from Singapore, I arrived at Heathrow, and Emily was there to meet me. Emily and I had become friends when we worked as secretaries for an import and export company in Liverpool which was close to the famous Royal Liver Building at the Pier Head. The two equally famous liver birds stand atop the Royal Liver Building and are mythical birds that represent the cormorant. Over 800 years ago, in 1207, King John was granted a royal charter to register Liverpool as an official town. He wanted a special seal, different from what featured on other deeds, and so he chose a mythical liver bird as part of the crest; and as such, the liver bird became the symbol of the city of Liverpool. The liver bird is also the mascot of our fabulous Liverpool Football Club and even features on Sir Paul McCartney's coat of arms, granted to him in 2001 on his fifty-ninth birthday. As one might expect, the cormorant has one of its claws clutching a guitar.

Designed by Walter Aubrey Thomas, the foundation stone for the Royal Liver Building was laid in 1908 and was completed in 1911 at a cost of 800,000 pounds. The main roof stands at 167 feet, with the spires reaching 322 feet, where the liver birds are perched. The female liver bird, Bella, looks out to the river Mersey, protecting the port and all those out at sea, while the male liver bird, Bertie, looks over the city, protecting the seafarers' families and citizens. The liver birds stand eighteen feet tall, and each of them has a wingspan of twenty-four feet. There are over 100 liver birds to be found in and around the city of Liverpool; Bella and Bertie, however, are the most famous.

For Emily and me, it was friends till the end at first sight, with both of us pretty much on the same page in many ways. She would commute to work daily on a ferry across the Mersey, and I guess we were liver birds in our own right as we lay each day on the grass parkland opposite the Royal Liver Building at lunchtime, eating our butties. We both worked in the sugar department and had more than our fair share of fun in the office. We became known as double trouble, so much so that we were separated by the powers that be, and I was sent across the hall to the meat department. It couldn't have been a worse move for me as, apart from missing my partner in crime, I had already started dabbling in vegetarianism. At the very least, if I could call it that, it was for the *office* side of meat and not in the disgusting slaughterhouse.

After we met, one of the first things Emily told me was that she was in an unhappy marriage and didn't quite know how to get out of it. They hadn't been married for long, but Dave wanted children, and she didn't. 'It's simple,' I told her. 'If you're both unhappy and can't work things out, you should give serious consideration to getting divorced.'

Emily and her husband, Dave, loved each other very much, and looking back, they thought marriage was what they wanted at the time. Both in their very early twenties, they realised that certain subjects should have been discussed before walking down the aisle. Initially, Dave had accepted a posting as an electrical engineer in the Solomon Islands; and with travel in her bloodstream, Emily was beyond excited, even packing their bags before the wedding. But immediately after they were pronounced husband and wife, Dave told her that he wanted them to start a family straight away, putting their travel plans on hold. Suddenly, Emily's dreams were quashed. Dave's decision sent them both in completely different directions, with Emily wanting to travel and dear Dave wanting to become a dad. Emily eventually had *that* talk with Dave, and they filed for divorce. Dave remarried soon after, making his family dream a reality, and Emily was free to pursue her love of travel. Both still remain friends to this day.

A few months after Emily's divorce came through, she moved to London, got herself an executive role in an advertising company, and lived in a groovy attic flat in Chelsea. My application to immigrate to Australia had been approved, and there was much to organise. Both our lives were heading in different directions, and before leaving the UK, I spent some time in London with Emily. She'd done a lot of soul-searching since her divorce, and I wasn't sure if it was due to her new-found freedom, which she had always craved, or the fact that she was an Aries, but there was no doubt that she was living up to her fiery star sign with gusto.

We spent many fun times in her flat reminiscing about our love lives, our jobs in Liverpool, and the wild, drunken nights we'd shared. We'd talk for hours, drinking ourselves silly with pots of tea by day and bottles of wine by night. Emily was 165 cm and very attractive, with a cute nose and a dainty mouth to match. She had shoulder-length blond hair and piercing brown eyes, the sort of eyes you couldn't lie to, the sort of eyes that could see through everything. She had a mind like a steel trap and didn't suffer fools gladly. We went to many wild and crazy parties and met many wild and crazy people. Well, let's face it, London was *so* conducive to misbehaving badly, and misbehave badly we did often.

Emily's smiling face was a sight for sore eyes as I finally emerged through customs. It was such a happy reunion, not to mention an emotional one for me, being back on Mother England's soil once more. Emily and I had missed each other a great deal after I'd immigrated to Oz, so it was brilliant to be back with her on our old stomping ground, just like the good old days – and nights. The two of us had already been to Lindos in Greece a couple of times with my sister Kelly when we all lived in London a couple of years earlier, and the thought of returning to our Greek Sha(n)gri-la excited us beyond the beyond. In fact, the first time all three of us went to Lindos, we loved it so much that, upon our return to London, we booked ourselves onto a flight the following weekend and went back for another three weeks.

I spent the night in Emily's trendy abode. She shared the flat with Charlotte, a very well-spoken girl who was an advertising copywriter. Charlotte was around 175 cm and slim and had short brown hair that she spiked with wax, and she was gorgeous. She wore hip London fashion and had it all going on. She loved a good get-together with nibbles and wine, and we all wished she was coming with us to Greece, but the agency needed her for some high-profile job.

I opened my bottle of airline gin, courtesy of my dreamy purser, and proceeded to tell Emily and Charlotte about my sexually ill-fated night with him. Neither of them could believe that I'd let such a hunk of a man slip through my fingers. Of course, I agreed with them a million per cent and, still consumed with regret, offered reassurance that I'd be making up for my carnal faux pas over the coming months. 'Well said, and *that* deserves a toast,' seconded Emily. She organised some food and we spent the evening bringing one another up to date with our lives.

'Chinky cheers, Miss Flurry, it's so wonderful to see you again,' toasted Emily

'And here's to eroticism in Europe,' she added saucily. We cheered to that as we clinked our glasses.

Emily never called me by my first name. It was either Miss Flurry, the surname inadvertently typed on Kelly's and my airline tickets the very first time we all flew to Greece together, or LAF, my initials, which never failed to amuse us. In turn, I simply called her by her first and last initials, ER, which I would use in emergency situations; and of course, let's not overlook the royal connotations there, especially as Emily coincidentally was a sworn monarchist. I also called her Em or Emmy, which alluded to her outstanding performances in countless cardinal and comical situations. The evening was a long-overdue get-together, and we celebrated our forever friendship into the early hours.

CHAPTER TEN

I AWOKE TO A warm and sultry London summer morning. The sky was blue, and lust was in the air, a perfect day for a flight to the Greek islands. Our plane wasn't scheduled to leave until the afternoon, which suited me perfectly as I still had a few last-minute things to do. I also desperately needed to wax my bikini line. I stopped for a moment and wondered if that was another subconscious reason I hadn't invited the purser into my room that night in Singapore.

Oh god, the very thought of that gorgeous man and the very thought of me knocking him back. You know that feeling you have sometimes when you just want to kill yourself? Well, not literally to kill yourself but to give yourself a real bollocking over something you did or, in this case, didn't do, more's the pity. Anyway, that was then; this was now.

I dashed to the shops for some girly stuff and arrived back with enough time to wax the all-important areas. I had never actually waxed my bikini line before and thought it would be a simple enough task. I read the instructions and placed the strips over the unwanted pubes. After they'd been on for the required amount of time, I felt myself wince in anticipation of imminent pain. *Come on, don't be a wimp. Millions of women do this every day*, I told my cowardly self, but every time I went in for the rip, the thought of inflicting such probable ridiculous pain on myself for the sake of smooth, hairless skin just wasn't doing it for me.

Why had I thought I could do this? I asked myself.

'ER!' I screamed in a panic. 'Help!'

Emily had come racing into the bathroom, wondering what on earth I was shrieking about, when she stopped in her tracks, a witness to my most vulnerable of states as I stood there in my altogether, with strips of wax at the top of each leg and on the underneath bits. The longer Emily laughed, the longer the strips of wax were on my privates doing their worst. 'Get them off me, Emmy,' I pleaded.

Emily walked assuredly towards me and sat on the edge of the bath. I knew she was trying her absolute hardest to keep a straight face. 'Okay, LAF, no prob, you just need to pull the outer skin really tightly, hold it in place, and take a deep breath.' Emily looked up at my frightened face. 'And close your eyes so you can't see what I'm doing.'

Apart from my horrendous situation quickly turning into a complete nightmare, Emily calling me LAF at that very moment suddenly lightened my load and sent me into uncontrollable hysterics. Perhaps Emily might've been of some use had she not also been completely blinded by tears of hysterical laughter. To die laughing came close for both of us. The strips of wax had now been on for well over half an hour, and I envisaged myself on the beach in Greece with third-degree bikini line burns. So with absolutely no help from my unsympathetic friend, I very slowly peeled off the strips, which took forever and, in all probability, hurt more than had I ripped them off hastily in the first place. Never again would I indulge in this barbaric practice, and I asked God to bless the person responsible for inventing the humble razor blade.

Emily was all packed. It was now time to head back to the airport, stopping along the way to pick up Ashley and Maggie. I hadn't met the other two girls before, but apparently, they were heaps of fun and 110 per cent in hot pursuit of summer 'luurrvve'. *Look out, you Greek boys*, I thought as the four of us headed to Gatwick International Airport.

We checked ourselves and our suitcases in at the departure desk and, with time to spare before boarding, headed to the bar and toasted our holiday with gin and tonics. At the next table, a group of footy players in their twenties were downing beers and looking like they were in the mood for more than just fun. We wondered where they were going and if they'd get there in one piece. It felt good to be going back to Lindos, especially with Emily. We had some history there.

The plane was full of happy holidaymakers heading to brighter shores. Two weeks of sun, sand, and sex was on the menu for most of them and not necessarily in that order. I'd always believed that two weeks was never enough time to completely let go and enjoy oneself. You work hard all year and get two lousy weeks off in summer. I thought how lucky Brooke, Claire, and I were, travelling for six months and not just visiting the Greek islands but a lot more of Europe as well.

Ashley and Maggie were indeed fun, friendly girls, and as soon as we were airborne, we ordered more gin and tonics. The mood on the plane was relaxed and happy. There were couples off on romantic getaways, families looking forward to spending quality time together, singles wondering what was in store for them, and others just hoping for the best. Lo and behold, not even an hour into the flight, the group of footy players we'd encountered in the departure lounge had obviously downed a few more beers on the plane and were now singing footy songs, making themselves known to all on board. This was going to be an interesting plane ride.

After a couple of drinks, the four of us were ready to have some fun. Emily and I strolled down the plane, where we met up with the melodic soccer club, who invited us to join them. They seemed a little worse for wear but harmless enough. They'd had a good season and were obviously getting themselves in the mood for a well-earned, fun-filled, sexed-up vacation. Emily and I chatted and joked with a couple of the players for the rest of the journey, standing with them in the aisle. They were staying at one of the larger hotels in Rhodes and had drunkenly insisted on giving us their contact details, not that we had any intention of hooking up with them as Emily and I had other plans – plans that would be put into action shortly after our arrival in Lindos. Nonetheless, having some innocent fun with the guys on the plane was a good start to our holiday.

Ashley and Maggie were more than happy chatting to the two good-looking guys sitting in front of them. Ashley was a merchandiser in a luxury department store and had the gift of the gab. She was around 170 cm and attractive and had long blond hair, brown eyes, and a great figure to match. She loved playing sport and apparently was one of the top swimmers at school. I could only imagine how fabulous she'd look in her bikini down at the beach. She was bright and bubbly, and I knew she'd have no trouble finding holiday romance, and by the way things were progressing with the two guys in front, I think both girls had already found it.

Maggie was around 165 cm, had shoulder-length auburn hair, and was more petite in stature than Ashley. She certainly looked like she was in need of a holiday. She had a pretty face and green eyes and worked as a personal assistant for the sales director in the same department store as Ashley. She was a tad quieter, or so it seemed, than Ashley, but you know what they say – the quiet ones are always the worst. I got the picture that even though Ashley was initially more *out there* than Maggie, it wouldn't take long for Maggie to let her hair down once she'd completely forgotten about work. Both girls had never been to Lindos before and after a year's hard slog in the department store; they were both more than ready for two weeks of sun, relaxation, and whatever else came their way.

The time on the plane passed quickly, and before we knew it, we were back in our seats, preparing for landing.

CHAPTER ELEVEN

WE ARRIVED IN scorching hot Rhodes, the largest of the Dodecanese islands. Rhodes, or Rhodos as the Greeks call it, is a very popular tourist destination not only for the English and Europeans but, of course, for the rest of the world as well. In the old part of town, there were castles and medieval homes in medieval streets, surrounded by a medieval wall with 11 gates, although not all of them are open to the public.

One of the most famous streets in the old town is the Street of the Knights, which is about 600 meters long. In the early sixteenth century, seven inns were constructed in the street to house different members of the Knights of Saint John, who ruled Rhodes. The inns represented the seven countries from which the Knights of Saint John originated. The old town was designated a UNESCO World Heritage site in 1988, and even today, one gets a feeling of being transported back to medieval times when walking along this remarkable, legendary street.

At the entrance to the port at Mandraki Harbour, are the two famous columns, on top of which proudly stand the Rhodian deer, where the Colossus of Rhodes once was. The Colossus of Rhodes was a statue of the Greek Titan Helios (god of the sun), erected by Chares of Lindos in around 280 BC. It was considered one of the Seven Wonders of the Ancient World and was constructed to celebrate Rhodes' victory over the ruler of Cyprus and stood over thirty metres high. Fifty four years later, a strong earthquake toppled the Colossus of Rhodes, also significantly damaging the city. Rich in history and mythology, it was no wonder this beautiful island was so popular.

We piled ourselves and our suitcases into a taxi and headed to Lindos, which was about forty-seven kilometres from Rhodes. Lindos, a picturesque ancient village, lay beneath the impressive acropolis that towered above the little white box buildings, many of which had survived since the fifteenth century. Lindos was like something out of a beautiful old Greek picture book, having preserved most of its traditional Greek architecture. St Paul's Bay lay below the southern cliffs, where the apostle first landed, bringing Christianity to the island. It felt good to be back.

Emily and I already had Greek lovers in Lindos from our previous visits, so it wasn't presumptuous of us to expect that they would still be here, anxiously awaiting our return. After all, they had told us they loved us, and who were we not to believe them? The taxi dropped us off in the square, and we made our way through the gorgeous narrow streets and stone archways to Sophie's Place, where we'd stayed previously. Traditionally Greek, it was set behind carved wooden gates which opened up into a beautiful pebbled courtyard full of bougainvillea.

It was so good to see Sophie and her family again. Sophie's mother hadn't changed. She still screamed Sophie's name at the top of her very strong 95-year-old Greek voice. After lots of happy tears and hugs, we unpacked, showered, and changed, and Emily and I took the girls down to our favourite seaside, Pallas Beach, to soak up the Lindos sun.

My Greek was good. I could say 'Excuse me,' 'I want you,' 'I love you,' 'Come back to my place,' 'Thank you very much,' and 'You're welcome.' I knew how to say 'yes' and occasionally remembered how to say 'no'. Ashley and Maggie were impressed with my knowledge of the language and relied on me totally to organise their love lives during the next two weeks.

So there we were, all four of us looking fabulous and checking out the boys on the beach. It turned out that the girls didn't need any help from me in the love stakes after all, not that I thought for one minute they did, as Ashley soon spotted the guy she'd been talking to on the plane and ended up spending most of her holiday with him. He was a physician *and* a spunk, lucky Ashley. Mind you, I wasn't surprised she snared him early on in the piece with her good looks and figure. She loved a wild time and was about to get more of the same from the GP. So now we had a linguist and a doctor in the group. Maggie had, of course, paired up with the GP's friend and was looking more than happy with herself and, I suspected, had totally forgotten all about work.

We spent the whole day down at Pallas Beach, swimming and sunning ourselves. We lived on Greek salads and cocktails. The banana banshee had become our all-time favourite cocktail the first time we'd visited Lindos, and so the tradition continued. It comprised banana liqueur, white crème de cacao, fresh cream, and a banana, all perfectly blended together and poured over ice. A cocktail umbrella skilfully pierced through cut fruit on the side of the glass consummated our delicious beverage.

Emily and I discussed our Greek boyfriends and couldn't wait to see them again. 'Demetri is going to die when he sees me, Em. What do you reckon Yorgos will do when you walk into his bar?'

Emily was smiling as she thought about her lover. 'He may die also, LAF.'

'OMG, ER, then we'll both be holiday romance widows!' We laughed till we cried.

In the late afternoon, we made our way back to Sophie's Place. We walked up the steep hill, stopping every so often to say maa to the goats and *kalispera* to the locals. It was nice to get back to our accommodation for a lie-down under the ceiling fan to cool off. Emily and I shared a room that comprised two single beds, two small wooden tables, two plain wooden chairs, and a large wardrobe. Ashley and Maggie were in the adjoining room, which had the exact same layout. Our digs were simple and clean, and the four of us shared one bathroom, which was quite large. There was a communal outdoor kitchen with a large wooden table and eight chairs and a fridge, where we were able to store bread, milk, cheese, fruit, and more importantly our banana banshee ingredients, plus a couple of bottles of ouzo that we'd purchased in the village store upon arrival.

We took turns in the shower, did our hair and make-up, and applied sun-kissed blusher to 99.99 per cent of our bodies. We put on our sexy evening wear and agreed we all looked totally irresistible. We poured ourselves a drink, clinked our glasses with the traditional *yamas*, and then headed out into the balmy night.

CHAPTER TWELVE

I COULDN'T STOP THINKING about Demetri. The first time we met, Emily, Kelly, and I were having dinner in the restaurant where he worked, and it was lust at first sight. He'd brought the menus over to our table, and our eyes locked instantly. As he stood there waiting to take our orders, I could feel myself starting to melt from the heat of his body. He was tall with a muscular build, and I was mesmerised by his sexy dark eyes and chiselled face. He was clean-shaven, which enhanced his gorgeous olive-skinned features, and his long brown hair had been seductively bleached by the Greek island sun. His smouldering, handsome looks were akin to those of Clark Gable, my mum's favourite movie star. Often referred to as 'the King of Hollywood', Mum would refer to her illustrated book on Hollywood film stars, pointing out that he was the best-looking male star of all time. Mum used to say that she'd leave my dad for Clark Gable, much to the amusement of my dad.

Emily and Kelly had already ordered, leaving me staring blankly at the menu, unable to speak. 'And for you, *agapi?*' he asked.

OMG, he called me darling. I looked up and just stared at him for an eternity, marvelling at his exquisite male form. As he waited patiently for me to place my order, it felt like the planet had suddenly become deserted by all life form except for Demetri and me. The only two mortals remaining, we'd been hand-picked by the universe to make love morning, noon, and night, purposely chosen for an experiment to procreate until the world was once more replenished with humans. A new superstar couple was emerging, billboarded as a modern-day Adam and Eve.

Kelly kicked me under the table, snapping me out of my reverie. 'I, er, do you have something vegetarian I could have?' I asked.

'Of course, *agapi*, I will ask the chef to make something very special just for you,' he replied. His eyes never left mine.

'Efharisto,' I managed to say, the word barely making it out of my drooling mouth.

'Miss Flurry, that would have to be the first time I've ever seen you stuck for words,' said Emily.

'Yeah, are you okay, sis?' asked Kelly, feeling my forehead. 'Do you think you might be coming down with something?' We all giggled like teenagers.

Demetri stared at me for most of the night. Did he fancy me? Was he going to ask me out? Maybe I had tzatziki dip hanging off my face. Perhaps he was gay and just admiring my dress – he was certainly beautiful enough. 'Can one of you check to see if he's still looking at me?' I kept asking the girls. 'But don't let him see you looking.'

'Yes, he's still looking,' came my sleuth's reply. 'No, he's not looking now. He's taking someone's order. Hang on, wait, yes, he's looking again.'

After our meal – and a million glances between us during it – he brought the bill over to our table. Our eyes locked once more before he walked away, and I was completely under his spell. We each put our drachma on the plate, and as we got up to leave, he called Kelly over to the counter. *Oh no, it's not me he wants at all. It's Kelly*, I thought.

I raced outside into the ancient cobblestone laneway and quickly prayed to the Greek gods that he hadn't got the two of us mixed up. Kelly was suddenly beside me, delivering a message from him. 'He wants you to meet him here at eleven thirty tonight when he finishes work.'

I looked up to the evening sky. 'Efharistopoli!' I called out. 'Nothing personal Kelly, but I thought he might have been asking *you* out.'

'What? After tonight's Romeo and Juliet performance? No way,' said Kelly. 'Anyway, you know I've got the hots for Elias.' Elias was the local donkey wrangler. He was also a part-time vet, and Kelly was a sucker for guys who loved animals. I leaned back against the whitewashed stone wall, and tears of released joy – no doubt in anticipation of lustful sex later on that evening – rolled down my face.

L. A. FLORRIE

We went to Club Lindos, the open-air disco, and I danced the next two hours away, my optimistic mind and body fantasising over what was to come. Club Lindos had always been our favourite nightclub. The DJs played the best music, and the bartenders were steaming hot. I knocked back a few banana banshees as liquid courage for the kind of night I was hoping for with Demetri, and I found myself wishing the minutes away with only lust in mind.

Before I knew it, it was eleven thirty, and I was back at the restaurant, which was now empty of patrons, my entire body trembling with excitement. I walked in, and he flashed me his sexy smile as he was clearing the rest of the glasses away. I hadn't even had an actual conversation with this gorgeous man, yet here I was, completely besotted. 'Hello, *agapi*,' he said in his mouth-watering Greek accent.

OMG, you are sooo hot, I thought, staring at his gorgeous face.

'Kalispera. Ti kanis?' I replied.

He came around from behind the bar and pulled out a chair for me. 'I am happy now that you are here. Can I get you a drink, *agapi*?' He smiled.

'Yes, please, an ouzo would be lovely. Thank you,' I replied.

He put some romantic Greek music on and came back to the table with two ouzos and brought his chair close to mine. 'Yamas, agapi,' he said, staring into my eyes.

'Yamas,' I replied, and we clinked glasses.

'I am very glad you came back tonight,' he said meaningfully.

'Me too,' I replied.

He stood up and held out his hand. I reached up and grabbed it before he had any second thoughts. He led me to the small area in front of the bar, and we started to dance slowly to the music. He held me close against his body, and I could feel the strong, solid beat of his heart. We gazed into each other's eyes, knowing what was to come. I could have had him right there on the dance floor. '*Se thelo poli*. I want to make love to you, *agapi*. Would you like to come home with me?' he asked gently.

'Yes', I whispered back, my eyes transfixed on him.

He held my face in his hands and kissed me, softly at first and then hard. I was dying on the spot. 'Ela, agapi mu.' He took me by the hand,

and we left the restaurant. He put his arm around me, and we strolled to his villa, which was close by.

It couldn't have been a more romantic night with a million stars lighting up the evening sky, the warmth of the soft breeze brushing across my skin. My heart was pounding, and pure lust was oozing out of my entire being. This man truly was Adonis reincarnated. We arrived at his villa, and he led me upstairs to his bedroom, neither of us saying a word. We stood in the doorway for a few seconds, immersed in the moment, when he gently pulled me into his arms and looked down at me as if it was his mission in life to remember every inch of my face. His dark eyes were like those of a raven, and I wanted to dive deep within them, blending every part of my soul with his. He touched my hair like it was delicate silk, provocatively running his fingers down to my mouth, seducing me every step of the way, finally bringing his lips to meet mine. His kisses were slow and deliberate, and I felt completely weak at the knees. We kissed for an eternity, and I wanted him like nothing else on this earth.

His gorgeous strong arms lifted me and carried me to his bed. He undressed me slowly, like he'd taken private lessons from the renowned Don Juan himself. Or perhaps Demetri was a method actor, rehearsing his bedroom scenes for the next Greek love tragedy at the local amphitheatre. His eyes searched my naked body, tantalising me as he provocatively took off his shirt, revealing his muscular chest. He slid off his pants, and there was no mistaking how eager he was for me.

He lay on the bed next to me as his mouth commenced its journey of my entire body, his tongue gently working its magic way beyond my wildest imagination. My nipples were hard as he licked and devoured them, the sorcery of his hands leaving no part of me untouched. He moved down past my belly button, my arched body welcoming his every move. His tongue was inside me, licking me, tasting me, wanting me. My body was on fire, and my orgasm was seconds away.

He pulled me to the edge of the bed and, showing no mercy, thrust himself inside me. His huge hard penis went beyond all limitations, finding every nerve in my entire body. I watched his face staring down at me, his eyes darker than ever as he continued to push himself deep inside me, faster, harder, my body responding to his actions with equal desire. My ecstasy was unbelievable. Demetri was coming too, and the warmth of him inside me felt incredible. Our bodies were so in sync, and I knew then that this would be one of the most beautiful and emotionally charged experiences I would carry around in my heart forever.

Afterwards, we just lay in each other's arms. There were no words to describe what had just happened between us. Demetri was an amazing lover, and we continued to make beautiful, passionate, mad, crazy love every night until I left the island. The memories of our wild, uninhibited lovemaking sessions were still so fresh in my mind, not to mention in other places too; and now here I was, back in Lindos, hoping Demetri and I could take up where we left off.

CHAPTER THIRTEEN

THE GIRLS AND I had dinners fit for Greek goddesses. We went to a popular restaurant in the little square, which was one of the oldest restaurants in Lindos, and the food was delicious. They served everything from Italian pizzas to traditional Greek food, and there was something on the menu for everyone. I slipped away at some stage to seek out my Greek lover. I couldn't wait to see him, and I knew he'd be excited to see me again.

There was no sign of him at the restaurant where he worked, so I went to his villa and knocked on the door, desperate to reignite the passion. His sister, Katerina, came to the door, and she welcomed me like a long-lost sister. 'Lucy, I don't believe it. How are you?'

'I'm really well, Katerina. How are you? It's so good to see you again,' I replied. We were hugging each other when she pulled away from me, the smile suddenly draining from her face.

'How is Demetri? Is he home? It's just that I didn't see him at the restaurant,' I asked, somehow not wanting to know the answer.

'Oh, Lucy, of course, you don't know. Demetri is married now and lives in Rhodes with his wife and baby girl.'

I just stared at her, trying to digest her words.

'I am so sorry, Lucy. This must be a surprise for you,' Katerina said. 'Are you okay, *agapi*?'

'Yes, I'm fine, Katerina,' I said, smiling. 'I'm very happy for him. Please say hello to him for me when you speak to him and give him my congratulations.'

'Of course, Lucy,' Katerina replied.

I couldn't leave the villa quick enough and just walked around aimlessly for a while, trying to make sense of what Katerina had just told me. I guess my Greek lover had fallen for his leading lady from the amphitheatre.

I picked myself up, headed back to the restaurant, and poured my heart out to the girls. They were devastated for me, especially Emily, but told me it was time to move on and find someone else. *How can I possibly move on?* I asked myself. *Where on earth am I going to find a lover like Demetri?*

We left the restaurant and headed to Club Lindos. The girls showered me with banana banshees, hoping the alcohol would ease my pain, but it was only making me more emotional. My heart was aching, and I wasn't in a party mood. I left the club, went home to Sophie's Place, and cried myself to sleep.

I spent the next few days convalescing on the beach with the crew. Even the GP and his friend were counselling me, which we all thought was very sweet. My heart was mending slowly, and if Demetri was happily married, then I was truly happy for him. I had loyally dedicated the last seventy-two hours to his memory, a journey my heart insisted on taking. It was now time to let him go, and I thanked my holiday amigos for being there for me. I couldn't help thinking, however, that his wife was the luckiest girl in the world.

After a much-needed shopping day with the girls, we all had a fairly relaxing late afternoon at Sophie's Place as we knew the night was going to be a big one. The girls and I walked down to the little square and had another superb dinner at our favourite restaurant. We spent a couple of hours dancing at Club Lindos, where Ashley and Maggie caught up with their dates. It was 20 June, and the time was eleven thirty. Brooke and Claire would be in Lindos by now, and it was time to make our way to the Sparkle Bar. I was beside myself with excitement and couldn't wait to see them again and hear all about Athens.

Emily and I – plus Ashley, Maggie, and their Lindos lovers – had frequented the Sparkle Bar since our arrival, and the owner had fondly remembered Emily and me from our last visit. He would always give his patrons his customary Greek welcome, the kind of welcome that made you feel like you were the only person alive. We nicknamed him the Magic Man as, every night, he'd perform the most amazing wizardry from behind his bar, which never failed to produce gasps of astonishment from his customers. His cocktails were renowned for being a work of art, made with love, devotion, and flair. If you were female, you would also score the Magic Man's signature sparkler, which he would skewer through a piece of pineapple, attach to the side of your glass, and take a match to, lighting up not only the sparkler but the thrilled recipient's face as well. Although his bar staff were well trained in this technique, there was always something special about having your cocktail made by the Magic Man himself.

The Magic Man was a wonderful, entertaining host, and his bar was extremely popular. It was a couple of minutes to midnight, and I had one eye on the Magic Man and one eye on the door. The countdown was on, and right on cue, on the stroke of twelve, in walked Brooke and Claire. I'm sure they'd been waiting outside, watching the second hand, before making the perfect midnight entrance. Whatever the reason, my money was on Claire for ensuring all had gone according to plan. Banana banshees all round, courtesy of Richard, and we laughed and danced until sunrise.

CHAPTER FOURTEEN

BROOKE AND CLAIRE loved the village of Lindos, and they both had their fair share of admirers. They told me about the guys they'd met in Athens. So Brooke and Claire *had* found Greek lovers and, by the sounds of things, hadn't missed me at all as they brought me up to date with their Athenian antics. Both Ashley and Maggie were full on with their holiday romances with the GP and his friend, and they were the happiest foursome I'd seen in a long time.

Claire fell in lust with a local guy called Stamos, or was it Spiros? It could have even been Stavros? No, wait, it was Stelios – I think. Whatever his name was, I know it started and ended with *S*. He was a little taller than Claire and had a warm, friendly face. His physique wasn't so much like that of a Greek Olympian, but his manner and the way he treated Claire was all that she, Brooke, and I cared about. His brown hair was short, and he only had deep brown eyes for Claire.

Claire couldn't wipe the smile off her face for days from all the attention she was getting, and we were happy that she was happy. After Claire's first night with the man with the name starting and ending with *S*, she casually told us that he was the proud owner of a book on the Kama Sutra. Brooke and I nearly choked on our lunch and not because the man with the name starting and ending with *S* had *that* book but rather because of the laid-back and uninhibited way Claire told us. A new Claire was born that day – or the night before – and Brooke and I couldn't have been prouder. Claire went on to describe some of the more gravity-defying positions she'd tried, and as far as Brooke and I were concerned, the more time she spent indulging in the sexually creative, the less time she spent worrying. God bless our Claire.

Brooke's affections were lavished on a hunky man from Crete whom she met in one of the bars, and that smile of hers said it all as they created their own brand of 'cock-tail'. His name was Periklis, and he was 186 cm tall. He had a lean, muscular build and had sun-bleached hair and brown eyes. He looked a bit like a young Clint Eastwood and was incredibly sexy. Lucky Brooke.

Periklis literally stole Brooke's mind, body, and soul. She would arrive back at Sophie's Place in the late morning, looking like she'd been partying for days. Of course, she'd only been partying with Periklis the night before. She told us about the romance of him, the sexuality of him, and the kindness of him. She told us that he would literally worship her entire body, starting from her toes, which he would kiss individually, working his way up to her legs and thighs – and everything in between – up past her midriff to her breasts, kissing and caressing them like they were precious objects of irreplaceable value – breasts, he prophesied, that would go on to nurture life itself. He would continue up towards her neck, biting it gently, playfully, and passionately until she couldn't take it anymore, urging him to enter her. But he would make her wait. He would kiss her ears, her eyes, her nose, working his way towards her mouth. He would lick her lips, entering her mouth slowly with his tongue. When Periklis was satisfied to the point where she was dying inside, he would enter her rhapsodically, bringing them both to climactic glory. Brooke told Claire and I that Periklis was heaven sent. We told Brooke that she was truly blessed.

CHAPTER FIFTEEN

EMILY HAD GONE in search of Yorgos, her Greek lover. Yorgos owned a bar called Socrates, and Emily had fallen for him the first time we visited the island. It was a popular place for sunset drinks, and so Socrates became our post-beach hang-out. The unofficial entertainment comprised an elderly Greek man who would dance outside in the street, arms outstretched, with a red rose perfectly balanced between his few remaining teeth. The Rose Man became synonymous with all the bars in the village, and he would perform his very special Greek dance each night for the patrons.

Yorgos and Emily were instantly attracted to each other, and he would ply us with free drinks every night. He told her he was a part-time sea captain, and he spoke perfect English. 'My dear Emily,' he declared the first night he saw her, 'like our Greek legend Helen of Troy, you are without question the most beautiful girl in the world.'

Emily was mesmerised as he continued, 'Your face could, indeed, launch a thousand ships. However, you need only launch mine. You will, therefore, come away with me, and we shall sail the seas together.'

Emily had been swept away by him literally. 'I declare he be nicknamed Yorgos Yacht,' she announced tipsily to Kelly and me in his bar one night. 'And I shall indeed drift away with him into the sunset, indulging myself in Hellenistic romance and untold banana banshees that have been personally concocted by his entourage of gorgeous male deckhands.' We raised our glasses to her very own Prince Paris of Troy and looked forward to imminent tales of the high seas.

The adventurous day arrived for Emily to set sail on her maiden voyage, and Kelly and I escorted her down to Saint Paul's Bay to meet up with Yorgos. He'd told her to bring a few changes of clothes in an overnight bag as he couldn't be sure where they'd end up. As we neared the shoreline, we were not only shocked but horrified to see

Yorgos preparing to anchor away on his small open craft, akin to the size of a life raft that would be carried aboard a cruise liner, oars at the ready. Emily, with her great sense of humour, declared that his name be changed immediately to Yorgos Boat.

The three of us were laughing uncontrollably when Yorgos spotted her and waved, motioning for her to come aboard. He'd certainly dressed up for the occasion, sporting navy shorts, striped singlet, and navy cap. Emily could hardly see through her tears of laughter as he helped her climb aboard his pride and joy. Kelly and I stood back and waved her goodbye as they set sail. 'Have a great time, Emmy, and take good care of her, Yorgos!' I shouted to them.

'There is no need to worry! My very own *Emily* of Troy is safe in my hands!' he shouted back, flaunting his muscles in front of her as he started to row. Emily was still doubled over with laughter, finally managing to wave back at us amid her nautical howls of hysteria. Although it turned out that Yorgos wasn't the majestic sea captain he'd perhaps led us all to believe, Emily was still well and truly head over heels in lust as, notwithstanding his very small vessel, he did apparently live up to his Greek reputation in other, shall we say, larger areas.

Emily's sea adventure with Yorgos had Kelly and I quite worried as it was now the fourth day since we'd seen her. We flounced into Socrates, declaring her as officially missing, possibly abducted by her prince. We also wanted assurance that Yorgos had proper safety measures in place to improve the security of such a small raft and that life jackets were also on board. The bar staff assured us that Yorgos would return soon with Emily, that he was an experienced seafarer from way back, and that he knew how to navigate the surrounding waters blindfolded. They also told us that their payday was coming up and the main reason for his imminent return. It was pretty obvious that they weren't worried in the slightest.

Thankfully, Emily did reappear that night, looking all the better for having been sun-kissed and Yorgos-kissed, amongst other pleasing signs exhibited by our adventurous new water baby. Kelly and I were relieved that their love boat had docked unscathed.

Emily's past holiday romance with Yorgos was coquettish and

exciting. Like me with Demetri, she wanted to resurrect the passion and adventure. Unlike me with Demetri, she was lucky enough to find her Greek lover still single and sitting outside Socrates, drinking his coffee, and chatting to everyone who walked past. Yorgos loved his bar and was there pretty much 24/7. He had a smile that welcomed everyone, and when he saw Emily walking towards him, he could do no more than grin from ear to ear, his eyes twinkling like they did when he first laid them on her. '*Agapi*, you are a vision before my eyes. When did you arrive back in Lindos?' he asked her.

'Oh, a day or so ago', she replied casually, not wanting to sound desperate to see him again.

'Well, my dear *Emily* of Troy,' he gushed as he embraced her and as Emily was dying multiple deaths inside, 'come and let's have some drinks to celebrate.' And that was it. The fire was rekindled, like they'd never been apart, both of them having left indelible imprints on each other's minds, hearts, bodies, and souls.

I was so happy for Emily and Yorgos. They were like a couple of young lovebirds making the most of the time she had there, which was just under two weeks of revived passion they would both now take pleasure in yet again. Lucky Emily *and* lucky Yorgos.

CHAPTER SIXTEEN

ONE OF THE many things I have always loved about the Greek islands is the vast population of cats. I have been an avid cat lover for as long as I can remember, having grown up with them as a young girl back in the old country. The cats of the Greek islands are in their multitudes and come in a mixture of colours from black, white, ginger, and grey to tortoiseshell, tabby, and multicoloured. They are young and old, long haired and short haired, long tailed and short tailed, some with no tail. Fed mostly by the locals, they are quite domesticated, even though they are generally not allowed inside the family home. You can always find a cat or two, or more, under the tables at Greek restaurants, hoping for tasty morsels or leftovers from kind and cat-loving tourists. I was, however, thankful to see that cat food and cat biscuits were available for purchase at the local grocery store.

You will also see dozens of cats down at the harbour in the early morning and late afternoon, waiting for the fishermen to return with the catch of the day. Cats can be found just about everywhere in Greece, living in harmony with the locals and the environment. This is how it has been for centuries, so whether you like cats or not, they are as much a part of Greece as the Greeks themselves.

CHAPTER SEVENTEEN

A FEW DAYS BEFORE Brooke, Claire, and I left Lindos, a strange but fascinating man arrived on Pallas Beach. He was tall and lean with long dark hair, pretty much the norm in Greece. He was drop-dead gorgeous and unusually dressed in a loose-fitting floral shirt, baggy army green pants, and thongs, with a headset glued to his ears. He was also the first guy who had remotely interested me since I'd heard about Demetri getting married.

He took long slow steps as he descended down the steep hill to the beach and would lean back at an acute angle, which looked quite hilarious from where we used to lay, to observe the daily goings-on. His name was also Yorgos. However, to avoid confusion and having unanimously decided that he looked like a modern-day Messiah, we quickly nicknamed him JCLA, which in our abbreviated holiday code respectfully translated to Jesus Christ lookalike.

It didn't take him long to approach our group. The girls knew I needed a holiday love interest, so they left me alone with him to soak up his mystical charms. He chatted me up like he invented the word *romance*, and after two days of outrageously flirting with each other on the beach, it was a foregone conclusion that tonight was the night. Brooke, Claire, and I were due to leave the next morning to catch a small plane to the island of Santorini; and seeing what was unfolding between JCLA and myself, Claire reminded me of our departure time. I assured her I would be there in time for our flight and that I had everything under control – well, almost.

JCLA was also a vegetarian, so I was over the moon when he suggested taking me to dinner that night to a popular vegetarian restaurant high up on the hill, overlooking the beach. Our mutual attraction was at an all-time high, and I felt sad to be leaving him and beautiful Lindos the next day. JCLA was so much fun. He was also very deep and meaningful and, for the same reasons as mine, had become a vegetarian because he loved animals and couldn't bear the thought of them being slaughtered for food. Our meal was sumptuous as we both enjoyed home-made lentil soup, followed by spanakopita, fried halloumi, and eggplant with Greek salad.

The setting was like a scene from a romantic movie. There were candles on every table and enchanting soft music playing. We sat outside in the courtyard and could see the starry night sky perfectly through the overhead vine. We drank far too much retsina, and as the alcohol travelled north to my brain cells, I was suddenly consumed with an overwhelming feeling that I'd been Greek in a previous life. In fact, I could see myself quite clearly – a Greek goddess, of course, adorned in a flowing white low-cut gown encrusted with jewels, bound at the waist with delicate rope, my long blond hair down past my small firm breasts, my feet and legs sexily strapped up in royal espadrilles. I had been worshipped and loved by all, and I had been especially worshipped and loved by Demetri and JCLA.

'Are you okay, *agapi*?' JCLA's voice brought me back into the twentieth century.

'Yes, *agapi mu*, I'm absolutely fine, thank you. In fact, I've never felt better.' I looked deep into his eyes, secure in the knowledge that we'd been together in a previous life and had more in common that he could ever know.

We ended up back at his villa, where he proceeded to undress, replacing his easy-on-the-eye nakedness with a white kaftan, looking like a unique mixture of Jesus and a sultan of swing. He sat cross-legged on his patchwork Turkish rug and sang mystical songs to me on his acoustic guitar. The furnishings in his villa were interesting, with nothing traditionally Greek but rather 1960s American hippy culture. We ended up in his bed, where we smoked some strange-smelling cigarettes and had our way with each other – twice, I think.

Unfortunately for me, I could never quite remember the finer details of our lovemaking sessions, courtesy of mind-altering substances, but I do remember waking up the next morning with the biggest smile on my face. As I slowly started to focus on my surroundings, I could feel the alcohol-related headache beginning to set in. I also had a terrible, sick feeling that I'd missed my plane to Santorini with the girls. My mysterious man was out for the count, but how divine he looked just laying there, his gorgeous olive-skinned body sprawled across the white satin sheets. If only I could have jumped his bones once more, but there was no time. I kissed his handsome, peaceful face and whispered goodbye.

I dashed back to Sophie's Place and finished my last bit of packing like a crazy woman. The girls told me that Brooke and Claire had already left in a taxi and would meet me at the airport. They also warned me of Claire's concerns that I was MIA. Poor Claire, forever to be consumed with worry. On the flip side, however, Claire now possessed – of which there was no doubt – more sexual prowess than Brooke and I would ever have. I said my hurried goodbyes to Emily, Ashley, and Maggie as they had a few more days left in Lindos before heading back to London, all three of them still enjoying their romantic holiday with their Lindos lovers. More quick goodbyes to Sophie and her family, and I was gone.

I arrived at the airport as Brooke and Claire were literally waiting on the tarmac, being called by the hostess to board the plane. I could see they were purposely dragging their heels, trying to delay proceedings, hoping that I'd make it in time, when Brooke spotted me frantically waving at them through the window as I was checking in at the small airport. As luck would have it, I made it by the skin of my teeth. 'I'm so sorry, guys. Too much retsina, a few smokes, and a hot and hippy Greek can play havoc with one's travel plans,' I professed.

'Thank god you're okay,' said Claire. 'I was beginning to think you'd burnt your bra and joined his counterculture club or whatever it is they call it.'

'Oh, Claire, I love you.' I laughed.

Then there was Brooke's huge smile. 'I knew you'd make it in time, gorge. I take it by the look on your face you had a great night?' she asked.

'You betcha, baby,' I answered, grinning like a Cheshire cat, or should that be a Greek cat?

Brooke and Claire were sad to be leaving Periklis and the *S* man, each of them filling me in on their last night of passion, with Brooke revealing that even if she never had another man in her life, she wouldn't care, seeing as Periklis had satisfied her to the *n*th degree in every way. Claire went on to explain to us in detail her most favourite Kama Sutra position, and who would've thought that she'd unexpectedly evolve into Brooke's and my go-to girl for future tips? God bless Claire as she delighted in her *out there* sexual experience, total joy written all over her face. Even her body was moving differently, more confidently. Her eyes, too, were reflecting her new-found liberation, and all three of us were loving every bit of this revolutionised, spirited sexual goddess. Happy and relieved to be a threesome again, we hugged one another as we set out towards our next destination.

CHAPTER EIGHTEEN

A SHORT JOURNEY ON a twelve-seater plane had us landing on the mystical island of Santorini. The Aegean Sea reflected the deep blue of the summer sky, and the sun was hot. Crowned with whitewashed buildings set high up on the cliffs, flying into Santorini was like gazing down onto snow-capped mountains. Our three souls were like that of the majestic eagle, soaring high above this beautiful island, hungry and anxious to land to devour its unsuspecting prey.

As legend has it, Santorini is also known as the lost Atlantis after a huge volcanic eruption in the centre of the island around 1500 BC, causing the greater part of the island to sink. The explosion also devastated the eastern Mediterranean, including northern Crete, the centre of the ancient Minoan civilisation. Some historians believe the Minoans were destroyed at that time, while others say there is evidence of them having survived for at least another 50 to 100 years after the explosion. The Minoans, said to be the first European civilisation, were enigmatic, educated people. They were self-sufficient with a huge maritime empire, trading with Greece, Egypt, and nearby eastern countries. Like most Greek islands, Santorini is drenched in history.

We climbed into a taxi, and the driver gave us a hearty reception. 'Welcome to beautiful Santorini. The view of our island from the sky is good, yes?' We unanimously agreed. 'You know, if you had arrived by boat, you could have ridden the donkey taxis up the 600 steps to the capital, Firá,' he said.

'You're kidding, aren't you?' said Brooke.

'Those poor donkeys, isn't that cruel?' I asked.

'What about all the heavy people they'd have to bring up?' enquired Claire.

'The donkeys are very strong,' said the taxi driver. 'It is no problem for them.' The three of us weren't convinced and were glad we'd arrived by plane, no matter how strong he said the donkeys were.

Our taxi driver was full of information and gave us a quick rundown on where to stay, where to go, and what to do. As we approached Firá, the main town, we passed the many colourful houses, churches, restaurants, shops, rooms, and villas to let. Mostly painted white with blue trimmings, there were some buildings boasting burnt orange and turquoise, some pale yellow and green. There were window frames and doors painted outlandishly red.

The taxi driver found us a nice cheap room for three, just off the main street, which was close to everything our uncomplicated hearts could possibly desire. We unpacked, and I nearly died from a heart attack – my purse was nowhere to be found. 'Oh no! My purse isn't here!' I cried, my voice trembling.

'Do you remember where you had it last, gorge?' questioned Brooke.

I sat down on the bed and racked my brains about when I last took money from it. I always carried some loose drachma around with me daily, leaving the bulk of my money in my purse, which I would hide in our room. It suddenly dawned on me. I looked at the girls and felt like a complete idiot. 'It's under the mattress at Sophie's Place.' I ran down to reception and rang Sophie straight away, who went to look for Emily. Thank god she was there.

'ER, I can't seem to find my purse, and I think I've left it under my mattress.' The panic in my voice was irrefutable and high-pitched.

Emily checked, and sure enough, it was there, under the mattress. 'Don't worry, Miss Flurry, I'll put it in my case now and take it home with me.'

'Thanks, Emmy. See you when I get back.' I couldn't believe it; I had absolutely no money, not that there was much in my purse anyway, but it was enough to see me through to London, sort of.

We held an emergency meeting, where it was resolved by both Brooke and Claire that they would each lend me some money. I voted against the resolution, knowing it was going to leave them both short. Claire especially had budgeted for everything in Europe and Norway, right down to the last cent, and that was due to her good account keeping. Brooke reminded me of the money Richard had given her, and that was her good fortune. I stood my ground. 'No, I'm not taking any money from either of you. I'll get a job washing dishes and motorbikes. I'll even gladly wash the poor, hard-done-by donkeys. In fact, there must be heaps of things I can do to earn some money,' I said earnestly. 'I can get a job in a bar making banana banshees. You know I can make them in my sleep. I could even get a job dancing on tables.'

My co-voters looked less than impressed. 'Come on, guys, you know I've still got the moves.' Brooke and Claire discussed the options I'd presented, but I was overruled; the motion moved 2–1. I felt sick to the core, but there was nothing I could do about it. I gratefully and humbly accepted both contributions and couldn't thank the girls enough. We all decided it wasn't going to ruin our trip, and with that in mind, we showered, changed, and headed to the nearest bar for banana banshees.

CHAPTER NINETEEN

THE ISLAND OF Santorini felt ethereal. In the late afternoon, it was customary for everyone to make their way to restaurants, bars, and lookout points located along the top of the cliffs to watch the sunset. The misty horizons in Santorini gave way to an illusion that the sun was a million times its size as it gradually expanded across the entire sky. It would then lure its awe-inspired audience into the most magical, breathtaking sunset ever imagined. If there's one thing that I'll carry around with me for the rest of my life – well, apart from Demetri, JCLA, a very special Italian, and a few others – it's a Santorini sunset.

In keeping with village custom, the three of us would sit at one of the clifftop bars, drinking our favourite cocktail and dining on local cuisine, and watch in amazement as the huge orange sun slowly turned the island and surrounding Aegean Sea into a deep red glow, the same deep red glow I imagined burning passions to be should burning passions ever be metamorphosed onto canvas. The spellbound silence from the crowd would become audible phrases of unrestrained effusion, some even applauding, as day dissolved into night. Before our very eyes, the once hot and untainted afternoon had brazenly turned itself into a sultry, sexy evening.

The banana banshees and Greek salads had served us well, and we were now on the lookout for fun. That also meant we were on the lookout for lust. The taxi driver had pointed out a popular nightclub that had a cave-like interior, so that was where we went. The decor was amazing, and we felt like we were in some sort of sexually provocative S&M chamber, not that any of us had been to one of those places, I can assure you, but one hears about such things. There were connecting walkways to other cavern-like rooms. However, should the last chamber be entered, it was predestined that we'd come face to face with several powerful and wicked mythical Greek gods who, without question, would worship, love, and adore us and then perhaps eat us, after which we'd be taken to the underworld where souls go after death. *Yikes! Hush with my limited knowledge of Greek mythology, why don't I!*

The walls and archways were whitewashed, with heavy contrasting dark timber tables and chairs and white trendy lounges strategically placed on the dark grey slate floor in the main part of the club. Romantic enormous white candles flickered in rooms and passageways, the gentle drippings of wax ultimately claiming tabletops and alcoves as home. The overhead spotlights were creatively subtle, and the atmosphere was conducive to sexual longing and desire. The music was European and seductive. And there was a smorgasbord of gorgeous guys. We found the best seats in the club, the hot waiter brought our drinks over to us, and we couldn't wipe the smiles off our 'cats that got the cream' faces.

We'd only been there for five minutes when three hot-blooded-looking males approached us. The three of us buckled up. 'Is okay we sitta here?' the tall dark handsome one asked Brooke in his sexy accent.

Brooke's dazzling smile spoke volumes. 'Sure, gorge, no problem,' came her instant reply.

The other tall dark handsome one sat next to Claire, which made her almost faint on the spot, and the other tall dark handsome one sat next to me, sending my hormones into a spin. These three guys were wearing exquisitely fitted jeans with shirts adequately unbuttoned to entice, and they looked like movie stars. These guys were unbelievably gorgeous, and they wanted to "sitta nexta us-a'. We couldn't believe our good luck. All three of them had flawless olive skin, dark hair, brown eyes, and amazing bodies. They were sizzlingly appealing, and they were Italian.

For the next few hours, the six of us chatted, drank, danced, laughed, and kissed, and the six of us were on heat. My tall dark handsome Italian told me about his home in Milan, that he helped manage three of his family's restaurants, and that he lived alone. What? This gorgeous man lived alone? I couldn't believe that no one had snapped up this stunning specimen of male, my time in Santorini getting better by the minute.

The Italians suggested we leave the club, so we just nodded and followed them like sheep. They took us to a beautiful restaurant, where we sat outside in yet another gorgeous, romantic Greek courtyard. They ordered a seafood, cheese, and fruit platter large enough to feed the entire planet and the finest red wine on the menu. The Italians were attentive and charming, and we were enjoying every waking moment of it. Every word their sensual mouths uttered had the three of us on the edge of our seats. Brooke's Italian was whispering into her ear with his tongue. 'We're going for a stroll, guys,' she announced, winking at both Claire and me.

'Maybe-a we go-a somewhere else-a for coffee, *si?*' asked Claire's Italian, his body language for all the world saying, *Stuff the coffee.*

'Yes, I'd like that,' she replied, dragging him away like I'd never seen Claire drag before. I got the distinct impression that she had some Kama Sutra moves she wanted to impress him with.

And then there were two. 'Perhaps-a you would-a like-a to come-a back-a to my villa where we can-a relax-a?' my Italian asked. I think my kiss answered his question.

We strolled back to his very expensive-looking villa, which looked purposely built for modern royalty and A-list movie stars. The interior was breathtaking, with jaw-dropping views across the sea. The walls and floors were not unlike those back at the club, with beautifully appointed lights creatively installed around the room. The white lounge was enormous, and I'm certain it was made from the finest of fabrics. There were colourful abstract paintings hanging on white walls and a sunken lounge on the far side of the room with floor cushions screaming, *Come and lie all over us!* They looked like they were made from Indian silk, and I pictured myself laying there in divine Do Not Disturb comfort for the rest of my life. The dining table was made from heavy dark timber and was extremely long, the twelve dark timber chairs ornately carved, also heavy looking. There were two enormous kitchens, one inside and one outside, the latter incorporating a built-in bar.

He invited me into the garden, asking me to make myself comfortable on the daybed next to the blue pool that sparkled under the beautifully arranged outdoor lighting. There were bougainvillea trees around the pool brimming with red and pink blossoms, with soft ground lights shining upwards to emphasise the shape and colour of the trees and flowers, casting a beautiful, romantic glow. My eyes could only feast on the architect's discerning accomplishments. The equally large outside dining table and chairs were also made from heavy dark timber and had been placed under the colourful vine, which had skilfully weaved its way across the patio roof, from the courtyard kitchen to just beyond the table.

He went to the inside kitchen and emerged with some tasty cheeses he said he'd found at the local deli and then sauntered over to the bar, where there was a sound system. The music he chose was sexy and romantic. He filled two glasses with red wine, kicked off his shoes, and unbuttoned the rest of his shirt so that I couldn't fail to see his extremely fit physique. OMG. He walked back to where I was lying and handed me my drink. As I sat up to take the glass, he sat next to me. I could do no more than indulge myself in this glamorous, provocative evening. 'Grazie,' I responded, staring deep into his sexy brown eyes.

'Saluti, bella,' he said, holding my gaze. One thing I did know about Italians and drinking is that eye contact is of paramount importance when clinking glasses.

'Saluti, bello,' I replied with my very limited Italian vocabulary. We sipped on the full-bodied wine and chatted about each other's hopes and dreams for the future as we both fell under the spell of the night. I pictured myself as his devoted wife in our huge Tuscan house, baking Italian bread and pasta in our huge Tuscan kitchen overlooking our perfectly maintained Tuscan vineyard, with five of our gorgeous bambinos all playfully pulling at my apron, living the perfect Tuscan family life.

He told me all about his mama, papa, two elder brothers, and one elder sister. He told me his mama taught him to cook and that his papa had passed on his knowledge of wine to him. His two brothers, who also helped run the restaurants, together with his sister, were all married and had three children each. He said his mama and papa had semi-retired from the business but were often in their most popular restaurant every weekend, lending a helping hand. From the way he spoke about his family, it was obvious he loved them very much. Mamma mia – I mean, could this guy be any more perfect?

He stood up and took my hand, asking me if I would like to dance with him. He didn't have to ask me twice as I fell into his to-die-for body. He was a superb dance partner, and we moved in sync to the passionate slow music under the beautiful Santorini night sky. His hands caressed my back, which was bare from the style of dress I was wearing. He ran his fingers across my shoulders as he started to kiss my neck. I leaned my head back, showing my permission for him to never stop. His lips were warm and desirable and perfectly shaped. I couldn't wait to kiss them again.

He must have read my mind as he took my face in his hands and gently kissed my eyes, my nose, and my cheeks. His finger traced the outline of my lips and slid it into my mouth, slowly moving it in and out. After he freed his seductive digit from my hungry mouth, he brought his lips down on mine. Our kisses were long and slow and then fast, tongues fierce, exploring each other's mouths.

I was nearing ecstasy already but wanted to prolong the passion. I pulled away from him and looked up into his enormous pupils, both of our mouths wet from desire. I moved my hands to the top of his open shirt and began to slowly take it off, marvelling at his gorgeous masculine olive-skinned chest. I slowly ran my hands across his skin and felt his hard, toned body beneath them. Another incredible night was unfolding right before my eyes.

I undid his sexy Italian jeans and knelt in front of him to take them off. And in less than a New York minute, there he was, standing in front of me, completely naked. I looked up at him, his head also now leaning back, giving me permission to do absolutely and without question whatever I wanted. I was pretty much at eye level with his equally gorgeous masculine, hard-as-a-rock olive-skinned penis. I gently fondled his manhood, slowly licking every inch of him. I heard him groaning as I took him inside my eager mouth, rubbing him firmly with one hand, caressing his buttocks with the other. His excitement was building, but before he completely let go, he brought me up to face him, his eyes completely wild with passion.

He stripped me of my dress and held me at arm's length, casting his eyes over my bare body. He kissed my breasts, taking each nipple into his mouth, driving me over the edge of desire. It was his turn to kneel. He ran his tongue over my belly button as he made his way to the top of my legs. My arousal was at its peak, and I welcomed the pleasure of his tongue moving closer. He licked me gently, bringing my state of frenzy to near madness. He knew I was ready as his perfect tongue inside me brought me to the most beautiful, longest orgasm ever. He lifted me onto the daybed and lay on top of my gratified body, entering me easily. He didn't hold on for long as he, too, came for an eternity. Afterwards, we lay together, happy and content in this magical moment, until we fell asleep.

We awoke under the warm, early morning sun, and he asked me if I'd like to cool off in the pool. My heart could think of nothing more it would like to do. We swam quietly together, the water gently lapping in and around our naked bodies. God, it felt good. He felt good. My feet left the bottom of the pool as he picked me up and held my weightless body in his arms. We embraced each other and the rapturous moment.

Our moistened lips kissed passionately, his now familiar strong tongue easily finding mine. He was hard beneath me, and I could do no more than surrender myself to this beautiful, sexy man once more. As he entered me, I exhaled every ounce of breath I had, and I was entirely under his control. He was holding me firmly, pushing himself back and forth, in and out, as he continued to give me orgasm after orgasm. His actions were becoming more rapid, his fingers digging deep into my skin as he anticipated his own beautiful ejaculation. He was speaking Italian as he exploded inside me. His ecstasy seemed to go on forever as my body continuously jolted from the full force of his powerful orgasm.

Afterwards, he lay his head on my shoulder, whispering to me again in Italian. I obviously had no idea what he was saying, and I didn't care. It just sounded so fucking hot, and I thought I'd died and gone to the promised land. Afterwards, he gently pulled me out of the water, and we lay on the daybed, his arms again holding me close.

For breakfast, he made freshly ground coffee and brought out warm croissants, cheese, and fresh fruit. He made love to me again before I left, leaving me with absolutely no choice but to learn fluent Italian, become a connoisseur in wine, take cookery lessons to become the best pasta al dente chef in the world, *and* immigrate to Milan to live out my life with him and our five beautiful babies.

'O mio dio. Grazie, bella' – some beautiful Italian words I shall never forget. He was Allesandro, a beautiful Italian man I shall never forget.

CHAPTER TWENTY

S O FAR, I had no regrets about the vow I made to myself in Singapore because I would have never ever, *ever* forgiven myself had I not spent the most unforgettable night and morning with the sexiest, most gorgeous, passionate, considerate, husband material Italian lover on the planet. Like Demetri – and probably JCLA, if only I could remember, dammit – his lovemaking was full of romance and passion, making sure I was satisfied in every way. Of course, it worked both ways, and I more than showed him what we British girls were made of. I came to the swift conclusion, from my own up-to-the-minute experience, that European men definitely had the edge over non-European men in the romance/love/lust/sexy department. Not only did they possess a natural passion for the best food, wine, fashion, and not least of all life itself but they also had an innate passion for love. Of course, there's also something really sexy about the male species conversing in their native language when making love, especially at the point of no return.

Brooke, Claire, and I met back at our room later that morning, quickly touching on the previous night's events. We continued our in-depth discussion on our gorgeous, red-hot lovers over a luncheon specifically designed for hangovers, which comprised an extremely tasty traditional Greek vegetable casserole with freshly baked bread. The Italians, sadly, had been leaving that day to return home to Milan, and the three of us were like dreamy schoolgirls who would continue to argue for the next three decades over who had scored the best-looking Italian, not to mention the best lover.

Our adequate, delicious lunch and full-on sexual topic of conversation was just what Dr Love ordered, and with bathers and towels in tow, it was time to top up the suntans and spend a lazy afternoon on the beach. We strolled to the square and waited for the local bus to take us down to the coast. The sun was boiling, and we were desperate for a swim.

When the bus pulled in, we could see that it was already jam-packed from the line of people standing in the aisle. 'You've got to be joking,' said Brooke. 'If I don't throw myself into the water soon, I'm going to have heat convulsions, and it's not going to be pretty.'

It was obvious we'd have to wait for the next bus when, miraculously, we heard the driver shout to the standing passengers, 'Move, please, down the bus!' Brooke's prayers had been answered as he let half a dozen or so more people on, including us.

We were standing next to him when, to our surprise and absolute disbelief, he shouted again, 'Move, please, down the bus!' He then proceeded to let at least another eight people on. I'm not entirely sure, but there must have been close to 100 people on that sardine beach bus as he hurtled down the cliff roads, oblivious to any road rules that may have been in place.

Those of us unlucky enough to be standing in the aisle and being thrown in all directions were holding on tightly to poles, ceiling ropes, and one another for dear life. It was hot and stuffy. Every window on the bus was open, which only served to let in even more hot air, albeit moving hot air. The music was blaring from the bus radio, and the driver was singing along like he was representing Greece in the next Eurovision Song Contest. I came to the immediate conclusion that he was either behind schedule and making up for lost time, although he didn't really seem to be the type who cared about such things, or he quite simply had a penchant for inflicting fear on the young and innocent. Nothing short of a miracle saw us arriving safely at our destination.

By the time everyone disembarked, I'm sure the three of us weren't the only ones thanking the Greek gods – the non people-eating ones, of course – for having survived the scariest bus ride ever known to man, woman, and child. After a short and unsteady 'we can't believe we're still alive' walk across the road to the beach, we lay down on our towels, still offering thanks to the compassionate gods for sparing our young lives. 'I'm sure I would've thrown up had we been on that bus a minute longer,' declared Brooke.

'Me too,' replied Claire and I in unison.

'Tell me again why we drank so much last night?' asked Claire.

'The Italians', both Brooke and I replied. The three of us let out dreamy sighs, promptly followed by a minute's silence to ponder the previous night's passionate dalliances.

The dark volcanic sand was hot and coarse beneath our feet as we ran across what felt like burning coals, until we reached the crystal clear blue sea to cool down. We swam, sunbathed, and slept. Of course, as one would expect on a Greek island beach, there were lots of desirable European men to be looked at and admired and, perhaps more importantly, to be had. However, we had no complaints with regard to our accomplishments to date; and although we were young and constantly on heat from the summer sun, there comes a time when one has to slow down, take a breath, and reflect. And reflect we did for the rest of the day – on the Italians.

By the time we left the beach, we were feeling great, our hangovers were pretty much non-existent, and our tans were coming along nicely. The three of us couldn't wait to explore this gorgeous island, unanimous in our decision that it wasn't going to be with the local bus company. We caught a taxi back to our room, showered and changed, and had a quiet dinner in our favourite clifftop bar, marvelling again at the spectacular Santorini sunset, followed by an early night.

The next morning, we hired three motorbikes and headed north to Oia, pronounced *eeya*. Our well-informed taxi driver had told us it was a must-do excursion and that there was no better way to travel to Oia than by motorbike. Indeed, our road trip to Oia was breathtaking as we passed little blue domed churches, brightly painted art galleries, sparkling jewellery shops, delectable cafes, and enchanting whitewashed villas, all set against the backdrop of the resplendent Aegean Sea. There were masses of bright pink, purple, and red bougainvillea reaching out to us. We felt so free riding our motorbikes with the soft, warm island breeze blowing through our hair. In the past, I could never quite comprehend the love affair people had with their motorbikes and the feeling of total freedom they apparently brought. I finally understood their passion the day we rode to Oia. We could have ridden to the ends of the earth that day as we, too, found ourselves captivated in the realm of freedom.

We stopped for lunch on a rooftop restaurant, where the view across the Aegean Sea was surely that of heaven itself. Like paradise magnified one trillion times, the three of us were locked in tranquillity as we took in the majestic scene before us. How blessed we were at that moment.

After a more than perfect, serene lunch feasting on Greek salad, dips, cheeses, bread, and a nice crisp local white wine, we leisurely rode our motorbikes back to Firá along the cliff road, savouring every sight, sound, and smell along the way, our three hearts bursting with complete happiness and gratitude. Occasionally in life, we ask ourselves questions like 'Why are we here? What is it all about? What is the purpose of life?' I have to say that, for me, those questions were answered during my stay on the beautiful island of Santorini.

We were back in our room, barely able to speak, still in a trance-like state from the magical time and view we'd witnessed back at Oia. We quietly showered and changed, each of us going about our business like we'd taken holy vows of silence, the three of us made wholesome and pure again, agreeing without question that the last few hours had been in total contrast to our holiday thus far. Our visit to Oia had had the most profound effect on us and would become, without doubt, a day that we would always cherish and one more beautiful memory that would remain in our hearts forever.

We strolled up to the lookout and had another delicious yet peaceful sunset dinner in one of the many beautiful clifftop restaurants. Again, we were spellbound as we watched the transcendent sun arrange itself amongst the Elysian Fields, the rich colours spilling from God's artistic palette, swathing the celestial sphere in scarlet and deep crimson. We sat in our seats until the colour faded to black and then walked slowly back to our room, where we stayed until morning.

We spent a few more reflective days and nights on the wondrous, divine, and incomparable island of Santorini and were reluctant to leave, but our next adventure was beckoning.

CHAPTER TWENTY-ONE

WE TOOK OFF again in another twelve-seater plane and landed in Mykonos, 'the party island'. Mykonos earned its party title due to its similarity to Ibiza, with countless clubs, bars, great music, and its *anything goes* reputation.

At the airport, there were a dozen or more local guys holding up placards advertising their accommodation, all of them shouting at once, 'Cheap rates!' 'Best rooms!' 'Best location!' 'Best price!' Such confusion. There was no telling what their places were like or whose room rates were the best. Over to our right was a guy who simply pushed his way to the front of the crowd and said, 'Hi, I'm Nikos, and I'm the cheapest.'

'What d'ya reckon, girls?' asked Brooke.

'How do we know he's the cheapest?' questioned Claire.

'We don't, but we've got to stay somewhere,' I said.

'Well, he seems friendly enough, and I kind of like his cheekiness,' said Brooke, smiling.

And so there we were, in Nikos' courtesy bus, being driven to Nikos' Hostel. We checked in and, as requested by Nikos, surrendered our passports. I still don't know why we did that. He also made us pay for a night up front, no doubt before we saw the state of the toilets. He took us up to a modest room that had three single beds and a large wardrobe. 'Perfect, I can feel the fun running through my veins already.' Brooke laughed.

'Okay, who's up for the beach?' I asked, quickly changing into my G-string.

'Yep, I'm with you, baby,' said Brooke, changing too. We threw on our shorts and singlets and grabbed our towels.

'I'll meet you down there, guys. I just want to unpack and get organised,' said Claire with a hint of drowsiness.

'Claire, there's absolutely no time to waste on this party island,' insisted Brooke. 'You can unpack everything later.' But Claire being Claire, she stayed in the room and unpacked.

Brooke and I were on the same wavelength. 'You're right, Brooke,' I confirmed. 'There is definitely no time to waste on this party island.' And we were down at the beach in a flash.

The beach was full on, with hot-looking guys and girls in every direction. Brooke and I were beside ourselves with excitement, the island already proving to be more than we'd heard about and bargained for. We found a spot near the water, swam for a while, and then lay down on our towels to dry off and soak up the sun.

Brooke and I were discussing what we'd do that evening when an Irish accent interrupted our conversation. 'Hi, girls, how are you both this fine day?'

We looked up to find, standing before us, yet another God-given specimen of male. 'We're good, thanks gorge,' replied Brooke, flashing her trademark smile. 'How are you?'

'Yep, I'm good too,' he replied. 'Listen, my mates and I are just hanging out over there. Would you like to join us?'

I looked at Brooke, who was still smiling. 'Sure, we'd love to,' she said.

'Wow, that was a quick pickup,' I whispered to Brooke.

'It sure was, gorge,' she whispered back. We gathered up our gear and followed our new friend to where his mates were.

Brooke and I nearly fainted when we saw them, and it wasn't from the heat of the sun that was making us giddy. The other two guys were just as gorgeous. They looked at least five to six years younger than us, but fun was what we were after, and fun was what we got. We all introduced ourselves and chatted about common holiday adventures. The guys had arrived from Ireland three weeks ago on extended leave and had loved Mykonos so much that they'd put other islands 'on hold' for a while. We told them about beautiful Santorini and Lindos and that, when they'd completely partied themselves out, either one of those places would be perfect for relaxing. I had a feeling, though, that these guys weren't in the mood for easing up anytime soon.

They invited us for drinks to the bar across the road, where we took pleasure in their company for the next few hours. Brooke was certainly a match for them drinks wise, with my one to everyone else's two. The guys bought us lunch, and the liquid refreshments kept on coming. We told them about Claire and that it was time we got back to our room to check on her. They asked us if we'd made any plans for the evening and, after having the most fun in Mykonos so far, arranged to meet up with them later at their local pub, aptly named the Irish Bar.

We headed back to Nikos' Hostel and couldn't wait to tell Claire about the guys and that we already had the evening's entertainment arranged. When we got back to our room, there was a note on the door which read, 'Hey, girls, let's say we meet here around nine thirty to ten o'clock tonite and then go for dinner.' It was signed by Nikos. Wow, the locals were really friendly in Mykonos.

'You've got to be joking – a cheap room, dinner dates, and the luck of the Irish. It doesn't get much better than this, gorge,' Brooke quipped.

'Unless, of course, you're in Santorini with the best-looking Italian lover in the world,' she added. We both laughed and started arguing again over who'd had the best-looking Italian lover.

We burst into the room to tell Claire about the afternoon's events, only to find that she'd fallen asleep, all her clothes ironed and neatly hung up, her empty suitcase under her bed. We woke her up and told her about the Irish guys and the note from Nikos. That evening, we arrived downstairs on time, dressed to kill, when Nikos arrived, interestingly enough with two of his friends in tow.

They took us to a lovely traditional Greek restaurant where the menu was extensive and the prices dirt cheap. None of us had any romantic leanings or otherwise towards the trio but thought it was a really nice gesture for them to take us out on our first night in Mykonos. Nikos took over the ordering of the meals and wine for everyone. We were most impressed, and everything he ordered was fantastic. Even my vegetarian meal was amongst one of the best I'd had in Greece. We were all having a brilliant time, and the conversation and wine continued to flow. It appeared that being taken out by Nikos and his friends was, so far, enjoyable. Everyone was coming up to Nikos and saying hello, and it was obvious that he was well known in the community and, it appeared, well respected.

When we'd finished our meal, Nikos ordered the bill. When it came, he split it six ways and asked us for our share. What the? The three of us looked at one another, totally surprised that Nikos and his friends hadn't offered to pay for us, seeing as the bill in total came to the equivalent of around $30; after all, it was *them* who had invited *us* out. Brooke was not amused and reminded us that at least we had the Irish boys to look forward to.

After we'd all put our share of drachma onto the table and the bill was paid, Nikos suggested we all go on to a nightclub – the absolute cheek of the man. 'We've already made arrangements,' said Brooke in no uncertain terms.

'Where are you going?' asked Nikos.

'We're meeting some friends at the Irish Bar,' I said, incensed that he had the nerve to even ask.

'We'll come too,' he asserted, inviting himself and his friends. The three of us just looked at one another in total disbelief. We all left the restaurant, and the three of us hotfooted it to the Irish Bar, Nikos and his friends right on our tails.

'Can you believe these guys?' said Brooke as we walked faster.

We arrived at the Irish Bar, and there they were, the good-looking, fun-loving buff suntanned guys from the beach. Claire's eyes nearly popped out of her head. 'Very nice', she said to Brooke and me as we made our way towards them.

Nikos and his friends were still with us and stood awkwardly in the group as we chatted to the Irish boys. The three of us were trying to discourage the three stooges by not engaging with them much and wondered at what stage of the night they would take the hint. We thought it was pretty obvious that we weren't interested in them and that we'd never, at any stage, given them the impression that we were. Nikos even put his arm around me at one stage after his efforts with Brooke had failed. 'Why don't you come back to my place?' he asked. Was there no end to this man's presumptuousness?

'No, I don't want to go home with you, Nikos. I'm having fun with my friends,' I told him.

Nikos' two friends moved closer in on Brooke and Claire, the 'drachma dropping' as it became apparent to them, finally, that our affections were focussed elsewhere. Nikos and his friends eventually left, not happy chappies.

The Irish Bar was everything the guys had said it would be. The place was pumping with loud music and laughter. The bartenders were grooving to the music and skilfully juggling glasses. The alcohol was flowing through pour spouts on bottles from great heights, and the most amazing cocktails were being concocted. There were guys and girls of all different nationalities, aged from around 18 to who knows how old, drinking beer, liqueurs, wine, spirits, champagne, and cocktails. The vibe was electric. Everyone was happy, suntanned, and scantily clad, and everyone was looking for lust. The place was going off, and the Irish boys had welcomed us with open arms.

We were all having the night of our lives when Brooke and I realised that at some stage during the evening – neither of us sure at what stage, however – Claire had gone missing. It was quite out of character for her to actually leave somewhere without telling us, but we weren't worried; after all, Claire – who was still the sensible one – was now also masquerading as Aphrodite, the Greek goddess of sexual love. We might have been a little worried, however, had we not seen her pashing one of the Irish guys earlier on. It was apparent that he'd also gone missing.

At around two o'clock, Billy – the guy I was wrapped around for most of the night – and I decided we'd head back to Nikos' Hostel, leaving Brooke to her own devices on the dance floor with one of his mates. Billy was absolutely gorgeous. He was tall with an awesome body and had baby blue eyes with eyelashes to die for and thick brown curly hair. He had quite an innocent look with pronounced cheekbones, and as one would expect in a lad somewhere in his mid-twenties, no real character lines had yet been etched on his face. An Irish model in London, he was front cover magazine material. So both entwined, we made our way back to the room.

Wait, what if Claire is there with her date? I asked myself. *Or what if, as soon as Brooke saw me leave with Billy, she decides to race her guy to the room before we get there?* We had an unwritten rule – the room belonged to whoever got back there first with someone, while the others were banished to sleep or whatever under the stars or wherever. Hmm, the donkey patch was looking good, and I'm sure I'd seen the donkey man deliver some comfortable-looking bales of hay only this afternoon. But Billy and I couldn't wait and we ended up shagging each other's brains out under one of the outdoor tables at some restaurant en route to 'the patch'. I should mention that the restaurant in question was closed at the time, which of course made it totally acceptable.

Billy was extremely cute, extremely adorable, extremely attentive, and extremely young. The whole 'under the table' experience was extremely delightful and reminded me of my very first sexual encounter with Jimmy from high school, when we'd caught a ferry across the Mersey and climbed to the top of New Brighton Tower to have our adolescent way with each other.

After my quickie with Billy, curiosity got the better of me about his age. He was certainly younger than me, and I had, earlier in the day, put him in his mid-twenties. Imagine my absolute horror when he divulged that he would be 17 October coming. Holy guacamole, Billy was only 16! OMG! Why hadn't I asked him his age before? What was I thinking? Had I completely lost my mind?

My uncertain future flashed before me as I faced an unimpressed judge, a panel of disapproving jurors, and an overenthusiastic courtroom audience of twenty or so hot male models from the same agency as Billy, all cheering him on for his Oscar nominee interpretation of Dustin Hoffman's character Benjamin Braddock in the award-winning movie *The Graduate*. 'The evidence before me clearly states that the victim is well below the age of consent. It appears that you have forced yourself upon this boy in a sexual way, leading him astray in no uncertain terms. What do you have to say for yourself, madam?' the magistrate demanded.

'Well, in my defence, Your Honour, I was pretty sure, in my inebriated state, that I thought he looked 25, and I was pretty sure, in my inebriated state, that I believed what I thought.' Even in my over-imaginative mind, I knew I wasn't ready to hear the final verdict.

I brought myself back to the present moment, which was me staring unbelievably at Billy, horrified at the bombshell he'd just dropped on me. I blurted out to him a very abrupt 'I have to go' and ran back to our room without so much as a second glance backwards.

I got back to Nikos' Hostel, still in shock, at around two thirty to find Brooke sitting on the floor outside our room, laughing hysterically. It didn't seem like the right time to tell her about my age-inappropriate faux pas with Billy, and her joviality was a much-welcomed diversion. There was a second note on the door which read, 'If that is how you treat people you go out with, tomorrow, July 5, you look for a new place.' It was signed by Nikos. Brooke's state of hilarity was infectious, and the two of us were laughing uncontrollably, mine mixed with a nervous dose of Billy mortification.

We fell into the room, where we found Claire sleeping soundly but with telltale signs of a male caller having been and gone. We couldn't resist waking her up to show her Nikos' latest note. The three of us read his words over and over and were at a total loss about why the wonderful and well-respected Nikos of Mykonos would want to literally throw us out after one night? Okay, so Nikos and his mates didn't get their way with us, but we all enjoyed one another's company at dinner and, upon demand, paid our own way with a ridiculously small amount of drachma. Sure, we preferred the Irish boys, but arrangements had already been made to meet them before Nikos' dinner invitation. And like I said, at no time did we ever give them the impression that we liked them *that way*.

The three of us finally fell asleep from exhaustion, only to be woken up the next morning by Nikos himself, literally bursting into our room at eleven o'clock, screaming at the top of his voice, 'Checkout time, twelve o'clock!' The three of us just stared at him and, totally unable to contain ourselves, laughed louder and harder than when we'd first read his note. He stormed off slamming the door behind him. So one day and one night in Mykonos, and maybe the locals weren't so friendly after all. Brooke and I felt sorry for Claire, who now had to repack all her freshly ironed clothes.

We dragged our suitcases down the flight of stairs, and at reception, we found our three passports sitting on the counter with no Nikos nor staff member in sight. 'What, not even a "so long, girls, thanks for the memories"?' Brooke said with a smirk. Claire and I couldn't help but also smile as the three of us exited Nikos' Hostel for the final time. Brooke and I spent the next hour or so carrying our overloaded suitcases around the cobblestone streets, looking for another place to stay. Claire, also the smart one, had wheels on her suitcase, and I believe that was the only time Brooke and I were actually jealous of our Capricorn friend. We found another room which suited us perfectly, and this time, all three of us unpacked together.

I told the girls about my dire situation with Billy, and although still mentally scarred that he was much younger than I thought, Brooke confirmed, having worked in family law, that I hadn't committed an offence and that any alleged case before me be dismissed as should any thoughts of incarceration – saved . . . just. We discussed the probable ages of the other two Irish boys, and even though we'd joked at the Irish Bar that Billy looked a little younger than his friends, we'd still put them at around 25.

The rest of our time in Mykonos was spent dodging the Irish boys we'd met on our first day. It wasn't that we didn't like them; we did. It was just that teenage boys had never been on our holiday itinerary – well, certainly not intentionally. Much the wiser from my close call, the three of us decided that the more mature-looking hunks of burning love – at least 30 and above – would provide adequate sufficiency in any future lustful liaisons.

CHAPTER TWENTY-TWO

MYKONOS, ONE OF the more famous Greek islands, lay in the centre of the Cycladic islands in the Aegean Sea. From the fourteenth to the eighteenth century, Mykonos lay under the direct rule of the Venetians, who constructed a row of sixteenth-century windmills from stone to mill wheat. Back then, Mykonos lay on a prime trade route, its windy weather ideal for operating these types of structures. Each windmill was painted white to blend in with the rest of the buildings in Mykonos. The windmills eventually ceased production 400 years later, with some being renovated into houses and one becoming a museum. The row of windmills became the most iconic and recognisable landmarks on the island. They still stand proud up on the little hill above the town and can be seen from just about anywhere in Mykonos.

We walked along the labyrinth of narrow streets down to the central harbour, which was alive and buzzing, with fishermen working on their boats and passengers lining up to take day trips on ferries. There were luckier travellers setting off on private yachts, allowing themselves a lot longer than just a day or two to sail around the Greek islands. There were countless trendy shops, all profiting from an abundance of shoppers, and there were lots of fine restaurants packed with diners. There seemed to be an around-the-clock buzz in Mykonos.

White pelicans greeted holidaymakers at the pier and were tame and happy enough to be photographed, the pelicans that is, with all sorts of people. The story goes that Petros, the original pelican, was found wounded by a fisherman in the mid-1950s. He cared for Petros until he recovered, and Petros decided to stay. The people of Mykonos loved Petros dearly and treated him like the star that he was as he continued to charm everyone he came into contact with. Petros became quite famous, ending up on all sorts of merchandise, earning a great deal of money for the island, and so the locals declared him as the mascot of Mykonos.

We were told by one of the fishermen at the pier that when Petros was a young bird, he flew across to the island of Tínos and charmed the locals there too. The Mykonians, however, were not happy that the residents of Tínos decided to claim Petros as their own, and so they filed a lawsuit to get Petros back. It turned out that they won the case, Petros was returned to Mykonos, and the Mykonians celebrated with a huge party for everyone on the island.

After Petros died, aged 30, the locals were devastated. It is well documented that Jackie Kennedy Onassis, who loved Mykonos, heard about the plight of the people and donated another pelican to the island, a female called Irene, with another donated from the Hamburg Zoo. A trip to Mykonos would not be complete without having a photograph taken with the new pelicans in honour of Petros.

Like many of the villages in Greece, the villas, shops, and tavernas in Mykonos were painted white, the wooden shutters/doors and little balconies painted blue. Masses of other bright colours had also been splashed around, giving rise to the thought that only artists lived here. The narrow streets were carved out from pavers of all shapes and sizes, and whitewash had been used to painstakingly paint around each paver. Mykonos was chic and colourful.

From the harbour, we took a boat trip to Paradise Beach, where we were told all the beautiful and liberated people hung out. It seemed Paradise Beach was quite famous for a number of reasons, and we were certainly in for more than a drachma to find out what those reasons were. We struck up a conversation with a German tourist who told us, 'If you stay on the boat, the next stop is *Super* Paradise Beach, where the even more beautiful and liberated people go.' So naturally, we stayed on the boat.

Super Paradise Beach certainly was, shall we say, extremely full on and not for the faint-hearted. Absolutely anything and everything went on at Super Paradise Beach, and it was the first time I actually got naked in public, with Brooke and Claire getting down to their G-strings. We hadn't seen anything like it before on our Australian beaches. There were girls making out with girls, guys making out with guys, people making out with themselves; there were threesomes and foursomes and others just grooving to the music and, of course, lots and lots of nakedness. Wow, this beach was going off, and we were loving every second of being amongst these hedonistic, pleasure-loving, age-appropriate partygoers.

The atmosphere was gobsmacking, not to mention risqué, and everyone was, I hasten to add, beyond comradely. All three of us were propositioned more than once as one might expect on such a beach, and even though we were pretty much broader in mind than most, the thought of having or performing any kind of sexual act in front of numerous beachgoers wasn't quite up our alley, so to speak. We politely declined to get involved in the overt goings-on, choosing instead to just chat and cautiously flirt with these fun and free-loving nudists. Our conversations were pretty much the norm – you know, sex, religion, politics, and travel adventures, the first subject of which popped up in more ways than one.

I must say that being naked on a beach and taking a dip in the sea was extremely liberating, and had we indulged in drinking alcohol in the hot sun, who knows what we could've *opened* ourselves up to? Under the circumstances, the three of us conducted ourselves admirably at Super Paradise Beach; but in retrospect, perhaps we were all secretly wishing we hadn't. Whatever our thoughts – past, present, and future – a fascinating day was spent on that beach and one that will be etched in our three memories for a long, long time.

After a wild and crazy time, not to mention Fun with a capital *F*, we finally said goodbye to beautiful, exciting Mykonos and boarded a ferry to Athens. As we approached the gangplank, we spotted none other than Nikos, who was there with his courtesy bus, awaiting more tourists. We shouted fun-loving goodbyes to him, and as he was reciprocating, he suddenly stopped in mid-wave, realising it was us. We continued to watch him as he approached a couple of female tourists who looked in their early twenties. After a very short conversation, we saw their bags being taken to his courtesy bus. We laughed, hoping they weren't expecting any free dinners and who knows what else.

CHAPTER TWENTY-THREE

THE FERRY SET sail for Athens, stopping along the way at picturesque islands to drop passengers off and pick passengers up. It was just what our partied-out bodies needed, a leisurely cruise up to the Greek capital. We lay on the deck lounges, and the swaying of the ferry, in sync with the gentle Aegean waves, rocked us to sleep. An hour's rest was all we needed to recharge the batteries, and as soon as we woke up, we went for a stroll.

We were leaning against the railings, admiring the superlative view, when a man in uniform who just so happened to be the captain stopped to chat to us. We were telling him where we'd been, where we were going, the fun we'd had, and the fun we were about to have. Ten minutes later, we were on the bridge with him and three of his immediate crew. Memories of the Jumbo Jet and my purser came flooding back, and I smiled as I thought of him, wondering how many girls he'd fallen in lust with since our brief flirtation. Mind you, who was I to talk, not to mention Brooke and Claire who had loved and farewelled just as many.

The captain and his crew spoke quite good English, and my Greek had improved from thirty words to about fifty, so between us all, we conversed quite well. They were well-educated, fun guys, and all three of us were given personal instruction by the captain on how to operate and steer the vessel. At the end of our practical exam, which included each of us separately, with our hands on the ship's wheel – and which, of course, involved the captain standing behind each of us at the helm himself – he proudly announced that either one of us could navigate the ferry to safety should an emergency occur. He presented us with a bottle of his favourite red wine. 'A reward for being perfect students', he professed. We were so surprised at his lovely gesture and thanked him profusely.

He was somewhat horrified, however, that we wanted to open

the bottle and drink it straight way, immediately giving us further instruction that once the top was removed, the wine should be 'left to breathe' for at least half an hour before consuming. Well, it *was* hot, and we *were* thirsty. We obeyed his masterful knowledge of the grape and, as he wished, left it for thirty minutes, after which time he rendered each of our three glasses just under half full. 'This will allow the air to find the wine and will help bring the bouquet to success,' he advised. He sounded so cute the way he explained it. After breathing in the much-anticipated aroma, we raised our glasses to the captain and his crew. 'Yamas!'

We spent the next few hours cruising the Greek islands, like we were royalty on one of Her Majesty's finest yachts. Docked safely in Athens, we couldn't thank the captain and his crew enough for their wonderful hospitality.

We caught a taxi to the hotel where Brooke and Claire had previously stayed. Athens was huge. A cosmopolitan metropolis, it bustled with cars, taxis, motorbikes, buses, coaches, locals, and tourists. There were churches and shops and hotels and pensions and offices and restaurants and bars and everything. The old stone walls of the buildings whispered multitudes of stories from a bygone era. This antediluvian city was built around the Acropolis, upon which stood the Parthenon, the temple of the Greek god Athena, built in the fifth-century BC. Athens was truly monumental, and I was beyond excited to be in one of the most famous ancient cities in the world.

We arrived at our hotel, which felt colossal in comparison to the rooms we'd stayed in back on the islands. Brooke and Claire had kept the phone numbers of the two Greek guys they'd met previously and promptly rang them to arrange the evening's entertainment. At around six o'clock, the guys, plus one other, picked us up at our hotel and took us to a large open-air restaurant that had a massive dance floor, stage, and a live band. Our male companions were the perfect hosts, ordering a sumptuous hot and cold Greek banquet, followed by a large plate of cheese and fresh fruit. We drank lots of ouzo, and upon hearing the band strike up with the Zorba, the guys led us up onto the dance floor and, with their masculine Greek arms around us, guided us through the steps of their traditional Greek dance. We were having a wonderful time, and we danced for hours under the clear Athens night sky.

Brooke and Claire continued on into the night with their Greek dance partners. I wasn't interested *that way* in their friend; it was just plain old fun and a great night's entertainment as far as I was concerned. He was the perfect gentleman too, making sure I got back to our hotel safely. I hugged my male host goodnight, and he went on his merry way. I didn't see Brooke or Claire until the next morning.

The girls woke me up with their laughter and frivolity, and I couldn't believe how fresh and alive they looked as I'm sure neither of them had had much shut-eye. But of course, Greek food, local wine, dancing outdoors, and most of all Greek romance can cure most hangovers and lack of sleep. We had a quick breakfast downstairs in the hotel restaurant as we didn't have time to waste today. I was in for a treat as the girls had planned to take me to some of the tourist spots they'd visited previously.

I especially wanted to see the famous Acropolis. Known as the Sacred Rock of Athens, it is one of the most recognisable monuments in the world. I couldn't believe my eyes as I stood before this magnificent archaeological site and imagined what life would have been like thousands of years ago, a place of worship adorned with sculptures, a sacred land where the ancient Athenians would come to pay homage to their gods. In the depth of my soul and in my mind's eye, I could feel and see it all taking place before me as I stood transfixed, immersed in the lives of the people who had lived and died here, locked in a time capsule that had transported me back centuries. I was infused with a feeling of complete knowing and romanticism of these wonderful long-ago Hellenic people. *Yes, I was definitely here*, I fantasised, my role as a Greek goddess confirmed.

We went to a gorgeous family-run restaurant in the Plaka district, which had red bougainvillea literally climbing the walls outside. The window frames were painted deep blue, and the rocklike exterior had been left in its natural state. The twenty or so tables were all painted different colours, and all the chairs were white. It was such a sweet and charming place, its decor only enhancing our delicious meal, which comprised vegetarian hotpot, fried eggplant, dolmas, and tzatziki dip, accompanied by the best Greek bread ever baked and all washed down with red wine that had been left to breathe for the mandatory half an hour.

After our scrumptious lunch, the girls continued in their roles as tour guides, showing me around this quaint area, which was quite hilly and had a lovely village feel to it. Well known for food and shopping, the Plaka district was thronging with lovers of all things Greek. The girls and I admired the Greek architecture, old and new, and we carefully and respectfully trod the narrow old cobblestone streets, so typical of this beautiful country, and bought some locally handmade souvenirs. We walked some more around this divine place, a city so rich in history that just being there felt surreal. One reads and hears about Athens being the heart of ancient Greece, but it never really prepares you for the real thing – the real awesome thing.

Unfortunately, we still had to watch the money situation seeing as we were one purse down; so sadly, we only stayed in Athens for two days.

CHAPTER TWENTY-FOUR

WE HADN'T MADE any set-in-stone plans about where we'd go once we left Athens, so we just caught a taxi to the train station and checked the departure board to see where the trains were heading. We knew we needed to travel in a northerly direction and noticed on the departure board that there was a train due to leave in the next ten minutes for Skopje in Yugoslavia (now Macedonia). 'Let's do it,' said Brooke. Claire and I agreed.

We dashed to the ticket office, bought three tickets, and jumped onto the train two minutes before it pulled out of the station. We stacked our suitcases in the baggage hold and walked the full length of the train before we eventually found a compartment with an empty bench seat. We sat opposite three Albanian boys who looked in their early twenties – well, we thought they were in their early twenties – but with our – well, *my* track record, they could have been any age from 16 to 50. They couldn't speak a word of English but spoke German. I'd taken some German lessons years before and had a couple of Austrian boyfriends once, so I knew enough German to hold a basic conversation.

It was a long train ride up to Skopje, but we had fun passing time with the boys, conversing in sign language and my basic German. We found out they were on their way home after visiting Athens. The three of them looked like ragamuffins, and it was pretty obvious that their lives in Skopje were completely opposite to the lives we lived back in the land of plenty. Brooke noticed that one of them was wearing a belt with a Marlboro buckle, which became the topic of conversation. It was obvious he was chuffed that Brooke had passed comment on it, and we sensed he felt proud that he possessed something worthy of note. They told us they came from very poor families and that they'd been to Athens looking for work but to no avail. One wonderful thing that came out of sitting with these boys was that Brooke made the Marlboro boy feel important that day on the train, perhaps even forever.

After a long journey, we finally pulled into a huge train station. We were in Skopje, pronounced *Skopia*, and none of us had a clue about where we were in relation to the map of the world, apart from the fact that we were heading in the right direction. We knew nothing about the place other than we were somewhere in Yugoslavia. The Albanian boys had told us that Skopje stood on the banks of the Vardar River, and there was a stone bridge, probably built in the fifteenth century. We weren't sure if we actually wanted to stay in Skopje, so we put our suitcases in a lock-up at the train station and found a money changer. The currency used in Skopje back then was the dinar, a money so low in denomination that just changing $20 literally gave us dozens of notes. We laughed, fanning out our money like we were millionaires. How far from the truth that was.

Before we took a look around Skopje to see what the place had to offer, we decided to eat first. We hailed a taxi. 'Do you know somewhere we could have lunch?' I asked the driver in German. It turned out that many people spoke German in Skopje, and so my basic knowledge of the language came in handy once more. 'Ja', he said, quickly sizing the three of us up, motioning us to get in. Brooke and Claire got in the back, and I hopped into the front seat, seeing as I was the local interpreter, although it turned out he could speak *some* English.

He turned on his meter and drove for about fifteen minutes or so, until we arrived at what looked like a caravan park set back from a dirt track. It felt like we were miles from anywhere. 'The restaurant is here?' I asked.

He just looked at me without any expression whatsoever, 'Ja, it is here,' he replied.

I turned to look at Brooke and Claire, who looked just as puzzled as me. 'Well, you never know,' said Brooke. 'We could soon be dining at the best kept secret in Skopje. Let's check it out.' Brooke and Claire hopped out, while I stayed in the taxi in case it was a no-go and we needed to find somewhere else.

Once Brooke and Claire were out of sight, the taxi driver suddenly revved the engine and took off with me still in the front seat. 'Stop!' I shouted. 'What the hell are you doing?' He stopped farther down the road where it was quiet and started putting the hard word on me. I noticed he was rubbing himself through his trousers. I immediately reached for the door handle to try to get out of the taxi, but he grabbed my arm to stop me, bringing himself closer to me.

'My wife is away today. Maybe we go to my house,' he said, staring at me with cold eyes. I couldn't believe what was happening and what I was hearing.

'My wife does not like me to touch her, and I would like to fuck you,' he continued.

'What? Are you joking with me right now?' I asked, very quickly deciding that he wasn't.

'No, I am not joking. We can go to my house right now,' he stated categorically.

'No fucking way! Are you insane? You turn this car around right now and take me back to my friends!' I yelled, but he wouldn't take no for an answer. He put his arms around me and tried to kiss me; it was disgusting. His hot, sweaty, and desperate body pulled me against him. I tried with all my strength to push him away, but he was too strong. He was a solidly built man, and I was no physical match for him. I was absolutely terrified. His hand was fondling my breasts through my singlet, his other hand holding the back of my neck as he exhaled his sickening, foul-smelling breath onto my skin. I felt ill. He started running his hand over my bare thighs towards the top of my legs and was trying to get into my shorts. I was screaming at him to stop, clawing at his skin. I was threatening him with the police if he didn't take me back to the caravan park, but he wasn't listening to me. He was fumbling with my belt and started pulling the zip down. His hand was close to the inside of my bikini briefs, and I seriously thought I was about to be raped and disposed of by this repulsive, brutal, terrifying excuse for a man.

My mind was racing as my life was flashing before my eyes. 'My friends took your taxi number! We always do this to be safe!' I cried out as a last resort, mustering up all the mental strength and every ounce of breath left in me to fight back in some way, albeit verbal.

With that, he suddenly let go of me. He sat back in his seat, wiping his vulgar mouth with his sleazy hand, his breathing heavy and raspy. My heart was still beating at a million miles an hour, and I wasn't sure at that stage who was more scared – him or me. I was petrified, frozen to the seat as I watched him staring out of the windscreen, not knowing what was going through his mind or what his next move would be.

I thought about trying to move my paralysed body towards the car door handle so that I could open it quickly and make a run for it again when he turned to me. 'Okay, I will take you back to your friends but no police.' He seemed nervous but calmer, so I agreed to his unjust deal.

'Okay, no police, but take me back to the caravan park immediately,' I demanded, somehow feeling like I now had the upper hand. My luck was in.

He turned the taxi around and took me back but only halfway. He stopped the taxi and shouted, 'Get out!' I just about fell out of the taxi and ran towards the caravan park as fast as I could. He sped off like the proverbial bat, creating a cloud of dust behind him.

Boy, was I relieved to see Brooke and Claire waiting outside the caravan park, both of them looking up and down the track, wondering where on earth the taxi and I had got to. I was so distressed when I got to them, the reality of what had just happened setting in, that I just about collapsed onto the ground and started to shake uncontrollably, the zip of my shorts still undone. I told Brooke and Claire what had happened. They couldn't believe it, all in the space of ten minutes *and* in broad daylight. They sat with me on the ground, their arms around me, trying to calm me down. Brooke did up my zip for me and fastened my belt. 'It's okay, Lucy, you're safe now. You're back with Claire and me. Just take some deep breaths.'

Of course, there was never any five-star dining at the caravan park or any kind of reception desk. Bastard. The girls tried to persuade me to go to the police station, but the thought of sitting in a Skopjean police station for hours on end, being gruelled, and having to relive my nightmare was not an option. They probably wouldn't have believed me anyway. I was still in one piece, thank god, and I just wanted to try to forget what had happened. But I never did forget, and I still think about my ordeal to this day. I do believe, however, that telling him my friends had taken his taxi number actually saved my life.

Unfortunately, being in the middle of nowhere gave us no other option but to walk to the nearest main road until we could hail another taxi to take us back to the main town of Skopje. The three of us stuck close together. We'd only been in Skopje for about an hour and already had grave doubts about staying any longer. Of course, I was anxious and upset in the second taxi, even though all three of us were sitting together in the back seat. I couldn't wait to get out and was desperate for some fresh air. We were approaching the Vardar River, so the girls asked the driver to stop and let us out. Thankfully, he did, we paid him, and no questions were asked.

We walked along the banks and saw the old stone bridge the Albanian boys had told us about. We'd attracted quite a following of young gypsy children, who were quite taken with us. They followed us for a while, holding out their hands for whatever they thought we had. They were all barefoot, and the three of us wanted nothing more than to be able to buy them a lifelong supply of sensible shoes. Brooke bought some sweets that she shared out amongst them, much to their delight. God bless them.

From what we'd seen so far in Skopje and taking into account the latest sordid incident, there didn't appear to be a great deal to do or see in this town, and we were in no mood to go to the local tourist office to find out. The atmosphere felt strangely odd, not to mention foreboding. I was still pretty shaken up from my daylight kidnapping experience that we decided to get out of Skopje post-haste. The sun hadn't even set, and we were back at the train station, wondering where we could take our adventurous minds and bodies to next.

'I believe Split on the Adriatic coast is beautiful,' said Brooke, and the idea of being on a beach again was not hard to take. We found out there was only one train leaving that day, and it was going to Venezia (Venice) via Belgrade. They told us to try the bus station next door, and as luck would have it, we found out that there was a coach leaving for Split in two hours.

We immediately bought three tickets and then walked to the little cafe just around the corner. We hadn't realised how ravenous we were until we started eating. I was glad the decision not to stay in Skopje was unanimous as I kept having visions of being raped and murdered by the taxi driver and buried under a gypsy caravan, never to be seen again.

We arrived back at the bus station with time to spare, only to be told that the bus for Split had left half an hour ago, and they couldn't, or wouldn't, tell us why. We couldn't believe it – more bad luck – and worse still, they wouldn't give us our precious money back. We were now totally pissed off and so desperate to leave Skopje that we headed back to the train station and bought three tickets to Venezia via Belgrade. It didn't take long for our moods to change, however, from feeling totally luckless to becoming overexcited at the prospect of being serenaded to on a gondola by a handsome Italian tenor. And of course, we knew all there was to know about Italians.

We were told at the ticket office that the train to Venezia via Belgrade was leaving in one hour's time from platform 5. Perfect. We had plenty of time to get on and find some seats before it got too packed. There were a few people already on the train, and I boarded first to double-check with one of them to make sure that the train was, in fact, going to Venezia via Belgrade. Affirmative. The three of us dragged our suitcases up onto the train, put them in the luggage hold, and found a nice empty compartment.

We were already discussing the exciting time we were going to have in Venice when the ticket conductor appeared. 'Where are you going?' he asked in his lovely European accent.

'Venezia via Belgrade', the three of us replied in unison, proud of our pseudo-European accents.

He looked surprised. 'This train is not going to Venezia via Belgrade. You need the train on platform 1 on the other side of the train station.'

We panicked. 'Thank you,' we said gratefully and ran down to the luggage hold, grabbed our suitcases, and jumped off the train.

'Wow, how lucky for us that the nice ticket man came when he did,' said Claire, relieved.

We found a couple of guys who, from their attire, obviously worked at the station. 'Excuse me, please, where is platform 1?' enquired Brooke.

Without further ado, one of them took Brooke's suitcase, and the other took Claire's and motioned for us to follow them. I was left to carry my own suitcase. We followed them to where they unbelievably proceeded to climb down a ladder onto an empty train track, run across the empty train track, and climb up another ladder to the next platform. They did this across four other empty train tracks. Seeing as they were in possession of Brooke's and Claire's luggage, we had no alternative but to follow them, totally and utterly shocked at what they were making us do. Wasn't this in contravention of safety rules? 'What the hell!' shouted Brooke.

'Whose idea was this?' yelled Claire.

I had no breath left in me to call out anything as I was really struggling to keep up as I had myself, my handbag, and my heavy suitcase to negotiate down the ladder, across the empty train tracks, and up another ladder onto the next platform – four times. Even though we were in total disbelief about what was happening, it was actually quite hilarious, and all three of us started to laugh hysterically. My laughter was more like screaming all the bad stuff out after my loathsome, stomach-churning, and nauseating ordeal at the hands of the despicable taxi driver.

When we'd all finally arrived at platform 1, exhausted and still trying to digest what had just happened, the station employee who had been carrying Brooke's suitcase placed it down on the ground; came up to me, my hands still laden with handbag and suitcase; put his hand on my crotch; and gave it a good squeeze. 'What the fuck?' Before I'd even finished my expletive, the two of them ran away laughing, down, across the empty train tracks, and up again, and they were gone. 'You little shit!' I called after him, in German, of course. The three of us stood there, stunned and amazed, trying to make sense of the last fifteen minutes.

Whatever craziness had just entered and left our lives, at least we were now at the right platform, waiting on the right train, which was going to Venezia via Belgrade. We talked about the nice ticket man again, and had it not been for him, we could have ended up in Timbuktu. We'd been sitting on the train for close to forty minutes, and absolutely no one was getting on. 'Surely, if this train is leaving for Venice in less than half an hour, you'd think there would be other people getting on by now,' Claire said with concern.

'You're right, Claire, something's not right,' agreed Brooke.

We saw a different station employee on the other side of the tracks. 'Excuse me!' I shouted out of the window. 'Is this train going to Venezia via Belgrade?' Goodness knows why I asked another station employee as he would certainly be as untrustworthy as the other two.

'No!' he shouted back 'Your train is going nowhere. You need the train at platform 5!'

'No way,' said Brooke. 'What on earth?'

It was now pretty obvious to us that the train we were on wasn't going anywhere. We grabbed our suitcases and, because this was the only direction we knew, climbed down the ladder and ran across the empty train tracks and up the ladder again four times, finding our way back to the ticket office where they told us again that the train to Venezia via Belgrade was leaving from platform 5. This was now verging on the ridiculous, so we ran with what little breath we had left in us, our suitcases feeling heavier than ever, back to platform 5. By now, this train had filled up; and with only minutes to spare, we jumped back on the train. To be certain, we again asked one of the passengers 'Is this train going to Venezia via Belgrade?'

He replied, 'No, is not train to Venezia via Belgrade.' What in heaven's name was going on here?

We dragged our suitcases and ourselves off the train again when someone told us to get back on. Thankfully, the nice ticket man appeared in the doorway of the train, so we asked him, 'Is this train going to Venezia via Belgrade?' He completely ignored us and walked away. Again, what the fuck? The train was about to leave, so we thought we'd get back on anyway as it seemed, from all accounts, that this had to be the train to Venezia via Belgrade.

We made our way down the aisle, dragging our suitcases behind us, as the baggage hold was now completely full to the roof, squeezing past people who had standing room only, when we came face to face with none other than the 'maybe not so nice after all' ticket man. We asked him again, 'Is this train going to Venezia via Belgrade?'

He brought his face close to ours and screamed, 'Fuck off!' Okay, we confirmed it for ourselves – everyone we'd encountered so far in Skopje was absolutely and unequivocally 150 per cent insane, and right now was definitely a good time to leave. The whistle blew, and the train started to pull slowly out of the station.

Half an hour into the journey and delighted that each second was taking us farther away from certain disaster had we stayed a moment longer in Skopje, we managed to squash ourselves into an almost full compartment, still uncertain that the train we were on was, in fact, going to Venezia via Belgrade. The three of us were completely exhausted physically, mentally, and emotionally but managed to sleep, as uncomfortable as our seating arrangements were, for some of the journey. We awoke as the train was slowing down, and people were walking past our compartment in readiness to disembark. The train pulled into the station as we heard a male voice making an announcement. 'There will be a short stop in Belgrade before continuing on to Venezia' – finally, official confirmation that we were on the right train. The three of us cheered.

Skopje was now in the past, and not letting it get the better of me for the remainder of our holiday, that was also where I left the memory of the monstrous taxi driver.

CHAPTER TWENTY-FIVE

WE PULLED OUR window down so we could lean out to watch the chaos. Belgrade station was chock-a-block with travellers. We waved goodbye to the myriad of people disembarking and waved hello to the newcomers getting on. For a crazy second, we discussed getting off and having a look around Belgrade, maybe even staying for a day or two. For another crazy second, we voted against it, deciding to play it safe and continue on to Venice.

During our waving frenzy, I noticed an extremely attractive guy in the next compartment to ours who was also hanging out of the window, observing the madness. 'Wow, look at the spunk next door,' I said to the girls.

'Mmm, not bad at all, Lucy,' said Brooke.

I caught his eye, and he smiled at me. I smiled back. We exchanged a few pleasantries – in German – both still hanging out of the window. 'Möchten sie eine kaffee?' he asked.

Wow, that's the fastest coffee invitation I've ever had, I thought.

'Ja, danke,' came the fastest coffee RSVP I'd ever given. The train was about to depart for Venice, so we pulled the windows back up and met each other in the passageway. Brooke and Claire couldn't believe my good luck and thought it amusing that I'd managed to pick up a coffee date hanging out of a train window. I also needed to get 'back on the horse', so to speak, not wanting to become scared of every man I met during our trip.

He introduced himself as Alek, and we went to the dining car, where he bought coffee and cake for two. He was very good-looking, around 180 cm with a great physique, extremely short brown hair, brown eyes, high cheekbones, a noble nose, and extremely kissable-looking lips. His English was quite good, and we managed to converse really well. He was very sexy, and we were clearly attracted to each other. He asked me where I was from and which places the girls and I had been to so far. He wanted to know where I was from in Australia and was absorbed in everything I was jabbering on about. 'Well, that's enough about me. What about you Alek?' I asked.

Without missing a beat, he told me he'd just been released from prison. Of course, I was immediately taken aback, wondering what he'd been in prison for, and it was at that point that I wasn't sure whether to run or stay, but the heat between us had already reached boiling point, so no points for guessing that I decided to stay. I didn't ask why he'd been in prison, instead finding myself surprisingly turned on by the fact he was an ex-con. Was I of unsound mind at that moment? Yes, most assuredly.

He asked me if I'd like to go and find somewhere more private, to which I hastily agreed. He grabbed my hand, and we went in search of an empty compartment. He even offered money to the insane ticket man, who went looking for an empty compartment for us but to no avail. The two of us were so hot for each other that we ended up in the only place that was private *and* empty – the WC.

As soon as we locked ourselves in the small closet, Alek started kissing me, pulling my hair, biting my neck, kissing me again, faster, harder, more urgent. He just about ripped my clothes off and had me up against the wall with my legs around his waist. I thought I was going to die from pure, unadulterated ecstasy. The train was speeding along, and the vibration of the wheels staking their claim on the tracks below us pulsated through our sexually aroused young bodies. The wild rhythm only added to the excitement, the erratic movement of the carriages thrusting us closer together than we already were. His desire was unrelenting, and we were both so ready for each other that he entered me with the kind of force and unbridled passion I'd only read about in juicy novels. He was so hard and deep inside me that I could feel every part of his erection. I was so turned on by this whole spur-of-the-moment erotic encounter that it didn't take long for me to reach orgasm. Alek was coming too, blowing inside me like an erupting volcano that had been simmering for years, his moans of obvious gratification conveying pure ecstasy.

L. A. FLORRIE

We were both spent, and I wished for nothing more than a comfortable bed where we could both lie and bask in the glory of mutual fulfilment. It was obvious that he hadn't had a woman for quite some time, and I found his frantic lovemaking inspiring. Move over Mile High Club. Fast Track Club at Ground Level is alive and well.

Alek wrote his name and phone number down for me before he left the train, but I never did ring him, no point. That wonderful, exciting, and licentious act is one that I still think about to this day. I took a photograph of Alek, which is still in my holiday photo album, alongside his phone number.

It was a long trip to Venice. After Alek left the train, I had the biggest smile on my face, and the three of us laughed at me having lustful sex in the WC on a speeding train in the middle of somewhere on the planet with an ex-con. My vow to myself was back on track.

Hours had passed when a voice came through the speakers advising passengers that, very shortly, the train we were on would be splitting in two with one half going to Venice and the other half going to some other European destination. Of course, we were only interested in the Venice half, so our next question that we needed a quick and honest answer to was, which half was going to Venice? This had to be a joke, right? Apparently, train splitting was a regular occurrence on this particular line and one that no one had bothered to mention to us until now.

Panic was beginning to set in, but surely it was going to be announced which half was going to Venice? The minutes came and went, with no voice coming through the speakers to advise us of anything. The passengers we asked didn't seem to want to tell us anything either – typical of the last twenty-four hours. Just minutes before the train did its split, the not-so-nice ticket man ran down the train, shouting, 'The front half of the train is going to Venezia!' This was all very well and good, but from which point was classed as the front half of the train? Where did the front half end and the back half start?

'We need to grab our suitcases and run as far forward as possible with what little or no time we have left and hope for the best!' screamed Brooke. The three of us ran like crazy women with the time given to us. As we were running, heavy suitcases being dragged erratically behind us, we could feel something happening beneath us – the train splitting was in process.

Shortly after the commotion of the split, the part of the train we were on had secured its solitary status, the three of us still unsure if we'd made it far enough to the front half of the train. The good news for us was that we had because, a few hours later, we arrived in Venezia.

CHAPTER TWENTY-SIX

A N ANCIENT CITY with canals as main thoroughfares, Venice was indeed a sight to behold. Divided by the Grand Canal, famous landmarks included the Bridge of Sighs and Saint Mark's Cathedral. The Bridge of Sighs was built in the early seventeenth century, connecting the old prisons and interrogation rooms in the Doge's Palace to the new prisons across the river. The name, Bridge of Sighs, was given by the English poet Lord Byron in the nineteenth century, borne out of the notion that one could hear the prisoners' sighs as they made their condemned walk across the bridge, looking one last time at the outside world before being locked away in their cells. On a brighter note, local legend promised eternal love to all those who kissed on a gondola under the bridge at sunset. The three of us elected to see if this myth was true and were already on the lookout for romantic gondoliers wanting to keep the tradition alive.

We checked into a lovely boutique hotel, the receptionist proudly informing us that the Liverpool band Frankie Goes to Hollywood had stayed there. Brooke and I were impressed. The three of us shared a gorgeous room, and for the reasonable price, we couldn't believe our good luck.

The three single beds seemed comfortable enough as we flopped our tired bodies down on them momentarily to catch our breath. There was a huge dark timber wardrobe with decorative door panels and enough space inside for a truckload of clothes. There were a million coat hangers, which excited us like you wouldn't believe, and a large enough area on the top shelf for all three suitcases. There was a fancy potpourri hanging on a hook at the end of the rack which released a fragrance that reminded us of the bougainvillea we rode past to and from Oia, Santorini, on that majestic day. The telephone sat on an ornate small desk that sort of matched the wardrobe, and there was one old-fashioned dark timber chair neatly tucked under the desk. The bedroom window was already open, and from our second floor room, we could see and hear the hustle and bustle of everyone on the quaint little street below us, no doubt in search of Italian wine and locally handmade gnocchi, pizzas, and spaghetti.

We all unpacked a modest amount of clothes as we weren't really sure how long we would or could afford to stay in Venice. We showered and changed into our summer evening dresses and couldn't wait to discover the local eateries. We strolled along the narrow streets, flanked by quaint shops and cafes, and over the little ornate bridges until we found a fabulous restaurant overlooking one of the many canals. We managed to get a table right on the water's edge, and it seemed that the order of the day was pizza dripping in garlic. Famished and not giving any second thoughts to possible kisses from possible admirers, we ordered the largest pizzas on the menu. We were all extremely tired from the train scenario that we decided to have an early night. No one would have wanted to kiss our garlic-drenched lips anyway, so it seemed like a good excuse to get some well-earned rest.

After breakfast the next day, we took a walk to Saint Mark's Cathedral, also known as Saint Mark's Basilica. The cathedral, located in Saint Mark's Square, was consecrated in 1094 and nicknamed Chiesa d'Oro (Church of Gold) because of its affluent design, gilded Byzantine mosaics, and status as a symbol of Venetian wealth and power. Saint Mark's Square was full of people and pigeons. We bought some packets of mixed seeds and dried fruit from one of the market stalls which we shared amongst the gazillion pigeons and then did a tour of the cathedral where, from one of the balconies, we waved to our subjects in the square below. The grandeur was exquisite, and we had our photos taken in front of the Triumphal Quadriga (Horses of Saint Mark), a set of Roman (or Greek) bronze statues of four horses, originally part of a monument depicting a quadriga, a four-horse carriage used for chariot racing.

After our historic tour, we went for a stroll to the local shops. We stopped to look at some postcards on a stand outside a souvenir shop as it was time again to report back to our families in Oz to let them know where we were and how we were. As we spun the stand of postcards around, we noticed through the reflection of the shop window three policemen standing behind us, checking us out. We dug one another in the ribs and turned around to face them. 'Buongiorno,' they said. The three of us smiled as we 'buongiornoed' back.

'Where are-a you-a from-a, bellas?' they asked.

'Botswana', replied Brooke, ready to go into convince mode.

Claire spoke up. 'Actually, my friend is joking. We're from Australia.' Brooke withdrew from further comment. I could only laugh out loud.

'Wow-a, Australia is so far away-a. And are you-a enjoying your-a stay-a in Venezia?' they enquired.

'Si, grazie,' Claire replied. 'But we only arrived last night, so we still have many places to see here.' They were around our age, we thought, and very good-looking – believe it or not.

'As a welcome-a to Venezia, would-a you-a like-a to go-a for a drink-a with us?' they asked.

The three of us looked at one another. 'Well, they are cops, so we should be able to trust them,' Brooke said under her voice.

'Plus, they *are* Italian,' Claire whispered naughtily. We all knew what we were all thinking. We nodded in acceptance.

'That would be very nice. *Grazie*,' Brooke replied.

'Then please-a come-a.' One of them happily gestured.

They led the way as we followed them down and around the old narrow streets, chatting happily that we couldn't believe we were actually in Venice and now this. After we'd been following them for more than five minutes, Claire glanced at Brooke and me with that concerned look of hers. 'Where do you think they're taking us? Surely, one of the cafes we've already passed serves coffee or alcohol.' Claire was right.

'Mi scusi,' I said in my best Italian accent. 'Where are we going?'

One of the policemen reassured us, 'One-a more-a minute, bella, and we are there-a.'

'Okay, no problem, gorge,' Brooke replied with none of us any the wiser.

We eventually came to a little quiet lane, the policemen stopping outside a quaint building that looked like a boutique hotel, similar to the one we were staying in. 'Please-a wait-a here *un momento*' was their next request, and the three of them went inside. We stood there for a few minutes, wondering why they'd left us outside on the street.

The plot was thickening, and we were intrigued. We knew we hadn't done anything wrong and that our passports were in order, so being arrested for travelling on illegal papers wasn't an option. On second thoughts, perhaps they were friends of Nikos from Mykonos, who'd paid them a measly amount of drachma to track us down and interrogate us about why we'd chosen the Irish boys over him and his friends. Or maybe the abhorrent taxi driver from Skopje had finally been arrested for running a sex slave trade from the caravan park, and he'd grassed me up as the brainchild behind the whole sordid operation. Perhaps Alek from the train was, in fact, an escaped axe murderer, and we'd been brought in for questioning about his whereabouts. Then of course, there was the not-so-nice ticket man, who was an Eastern European spy, and we were about to be forced, against our will, to join his weird secret train sect. The questions remained. Who were these three policemen? Where were we, and why had they brought us here? We decided to go inside.

We walked into the reception area where they were all speaking in local tongue. The man behind the desk was shaking his head, his arms flying everywhere, confirming his Italian heritage. The policemen turned to us. 'We are-a very sorry, bellas. There are-a no rooms available for the afternoon-a.'

'What? There must be some misunderstanding,' Claire told them in no uncertain terms. 'We don't want a room for the afternoon. We already have a room. What we thought we were here for was a drink – a welcome drink to Venezia, at your invitation.' Go Claire. Wow, we knew the Italians were hot-blooded – from first-hand experience, of course – but this was ridiculous.

'I mean, it's one thing consenting and another taking advantage,' Brooke stated to Claire and me indignantly. Claire and I totally agreed.

We turned and left the hotel, the three of them coming after us. One of the cops grabbed my arm and had me cornered up against the stone wall outside with his hand on my crotch – oh no, not again. I grabbed his hand and pushed him away from me. 'Stop this. What is happening? Why are you doing this?' I demanded to know.

'I want to make-a love to you-a, bella,' he replied.

I looked over to where Brooke and Claire were. They, too, were being sexually harassed by the other two cops. 'You are crazy! All of you are crazy!' I shouted.

'Let's make a run for it, girls!' Brooke shouted.

'Like now would be a good time!' Claire shouted back.

We managed to break free from them and started to run back down the narrow cobblestone streets until, somehow, we ended up back at Saint Mark's Square, unbelievably with all three of them hot on our heels.

We were halfway across the square when this cop, this good-looking, trustworthy cop, grabbed me by the arm yet again and swung me around to face him. Brooke's cop had his arms around her, begging her to let him make love to her for the rest of the afternoon, and Claire's cop had his hands on her shoulders, trying to make her see sense from his point of view. It suddenly felt like we were all in a scene from some crazy romcom. 'Why are you-a running away-a from me, bella? I just-a wanted to make-a love-a to you-a,' he professed to me. One could be easily forgiven for being moved by his impassioned plea.

'I'm married with a child, and they're waiting for me at the hotel,' came my emotional reply, at the same time convincing myself that they were there.

'I want-a you-a, bella,' he kept saying, and it was obvious that he didn't want to take no for an answer, begging me to sleep with him, even though he knew I was married.

'Please, you must leave now before my husband sees you,' I pleaded. This was becoming Oscar nomination material.

'Okay, bella, I will leave-a, but please understand-a I just-a wanted to make-a love-a to you-a.'

'Yes, I understand, but this has to stop. You must go now.'

Brooke's smooth, sweet talking had somewhat eased her cop's need for an afternoon delight and Claire's distressed facial and body language had her rattled enough to threaten her cop with more police reinforcement.

After each of our stalwart performances, the three Italian stallions finally retreated, their tails between their legs, leaving Brooke, Claire, and myself questioning what we were doing wrong to attract all this craziness. We were back in our room, stunned at the latest mess we'd got ourselves into, glad we were safe from the clutches of the *Venetian Police*.

The next blow came totally out of the blue. Claire had decided to call it a day and travel up to Norway immediately to see her sister and family. We knew she was eventually heading up to Norway, but her plan was to go after we'd all arrived in London – together. Maybe she didn't think we'd make it to London, that perhaps after our latest escapade we'd finally meet our fate along the way and not make it to anywhere. No amount of persuasion would change her mind. We begged and pleaded, hoping she'd stay, but her decision was final.

Claire packed her suitcase, and Brooke and I walked her to the train station, still trying to change her mind. We knew that she was missing her sister and family who'd left Australia twelve months ago to buy a thriving fishing trawler business, but surely another few weeks of travelling with Brooke and me should take precedence? After everything we'd planned? I couldn't help but bring to mind the fact that I'd stupidly left my purse in Lindos, which of course had left Claire short of money in her well-thought-out holiday budget. Maybe that was another reason she felt she had to leave before her due time, and the idea of working alongside her sister and earning big bucks seemed like a more lucrative – and safe – deal.

Brooke and I made sure that she was on the right train. Or was she? We were all so sad it had come to this, but Claire was resolute. Our lovely, sensible, wise, and apprehensive Capricorn friend had finally had enough of the madness. Claire had certainly taken a walk on the wild side since we'd set off from Brisbane, but her adventurous nature, albeit recently discovered, had run its course. We waved her goodbye, the three of us inconsolable and broken-hearted, as her train pulled out of the station.

After Claire left, it wasn't the same in Venice, so Brooke and I decided to leave too, our shortage of moolah also influencing our inevitable decision to get the flock out. We packed our bags, headed back to the station, and caught a train to Saint Anton, Austria.

CHAPTER TWENTY-SEVEN

I GREW UP IN a working-class family in Liverpool and was the middle of three sisters. Elizabeth was seven years older than me, and I was three years older than Kelly. Louisa and Liny, my mum and dad, met on 29 July 1940 and became engaged shortly after on 16 November 1940 while Dad was home on leave from the Royal Air Force during WWII. When he rejoined his unit, they were sent to India, Malaysia, and Singapore via South Africa, where he and his mates delighted in swimming in both the South Atlantic and Indian Oceans at the same time. At the end of WWII, Dad would often think fondly of his mates, proudly recounting their two oceans' story, many times in conversation.

After a short stay in India, they moved to Malaysia and then onto Singapore. The war in the Far East was moving at a fast pace, prompting them to leave Singapore and head south to Indonesia. Heartbreakingly, it was during that move that they were captured by the Imperial Japanese Army in Java and taken to Japan, where my dad became a prisoner of war in Camp Hiroshima 6-D (Motoyama) for three and a half long years. Like hundreds of thousands of men who had all lived through such harrowing times in prisoner of war camps enduring deprivation and unspeakable mental and physical torture, living on bowls of rice, maggots, and only God knows what else, Dad came home a broken man, along with a health condition called beriberi, caused by lack of thiamine (vitamin B_1).

As soon as he was emotionally and physically able, he and Mum got married. Mum said that in the three and a half years he was a prisoner of war, she never looked at or was interested in any other man and had faithfully waited for him all that time. Their marriage was a match made in heaven. Mum told us three girls that Dad would regularly scream in his sleep after they got married. He never spoke of his time as a prisoner of war, instead uncontrollably reliving the deep-rooted and unshakeable hell in his nightmares.

Dad was one of eight brothers, and they all served in the armed forces. Only seven came home. Uncle Colin, the youngest of the brothers, was a merchant seaman bringing supplies from America to the United Kingdom when the *Oropesa* passenger steamship he was a steward on was torpedoed by a German U-boat on 16 January 1941. My grandmother received that dreaded telegram and was grief-stricken that her baby boy was never coming home. The family heartbreakingly mourned the loss of his young life. He was only 19. My grandmother had a framed photograph of Uncle Colin in his uniform on her bedroom wall. I can still see his handsome face smiling down at those looking up at him, each of us admiring his bravery, duty to king and country, and movie star good looks.

Once Dad had regained his physical strength and settled back in after the war, my mum roped him into The Spotlights, a non-stop variety show, of which she was a member. The Spotlights were a group of local entertainers who performed at many venues, entertaining the troops before, during, and after WWII. My mum made most of the costumes worn by the performers. Some of the costumes were made from blackout material, a fabric that was used primarily for curtains on windows to shield the light during air raids. Mum would often tell us stories of everyone running for their lives to take cover in the air-raid shelters when the sirens started up.

Mum was 21 when Liverpool experienced its worst ever bombing raid during the seven-night blitz from 1 to 7 May 1941. It was the most intensive sequence of air attacks on a British city outside London during the war. The maternity ward in Mill Road Hospital, where I was born just thirteen years later, took a direct hit on 3 May 1941 during this blitz. Landing in the courtyard at the rear of the hospital, the catastrophic bomb tragically killed many mothers and their precious newborn babies. Words could never describe the outpouring of grief and sadness from that dark time.

In The Spotlights, both Mum and Dad played piano accordions and performed as a duo. Mum was a dancer in the show too and also acted in comedy sketches with our Uncle Arthur, with Dad displaying his physical strength and agility in light acrobatic acts with our Uncle Harry. I have an album full of photos from their time as performers that Mum put together. She painstakingly coloured most of the photos with her artistic hand using special oil paint. 'If ever there's a fire in the house, the first thing I'd save would be my photo album,' Mum used to say, reminiscing about her days in The Spotlights. Her mum was also a performer in a circus, but sadly, we have no photos of my grandmother's performing days.

Dad found a full-time job some months after he was home from the war in a hot and sweaty tobacco factory. Mum said he just wanted to do an honest day's work for an honest day's pay. His amazingly tough, resilient body and acquiescent mindset that undoubtedly saved him from probable death in the prisoner of war camp would serve him yet again in that gruelling, unforgiving factory. For over thirty years, he rode there and back on his pushbike every single day of his working life through hail, rain, gale force winds, sleet, snow, ice, fog, and occasional hot English summer days, and I never once heard him complain. He was a good-looking man, tall with a strong, lean build. His torso boasted a six-pack and muscles on his arms that enabled him to straddle an open car bonnet and lift the entire engine out of the vehicle on his own. My dad was a quiet man and a real gentleman in every sense of the word. He was a loyal, dedicated husband, father, grandfather, and friend to all and had the patience of a saint. He loved and adored my mum with all his heart, and he cherished her, his three daughters, and his two granddaughters until his dying day.

In later years, Mum became a seamstress at the Playhouse Theatre in Liverpool, making costumes for all the productions. Her proudest achievement was making the costumes for William Shakespeare's *Macbeth*, which took hours of hard slog on the theatre's sewing machines. As the superstition goes, which is known as the Scottish curse, Mum told us that it was bad luck to actually say 'Macbeth' in the theatre, and so it would be referred to as 'McDougall' to avoid some sort of disaster occurring. Mum also loved to serve tea and coffee during intervals at the theatre. Mum lived and breathed everything theatrical, and when I was

13, she surprised me with a front row seat to watch *Romeo and Juliet*. English actress Georgina Hale played Juliet, and I couldn't take me eyes off her. My first taste of professional, live drama, and I was entranced.

After Mum eventually resigned from the Playhouse Theatre, she rented the local church hall on Saturday mornings and taught tap-dancing to the local kids. Every Friday night, she would roll back the carpet in our front room, and her students would all come to our house for extra lessons. She played the piano, as did Dad, of course, accompanying the dance routines she had choreographed, the very same piano that now has pride of place in my home in Australia. She taught several routines and made all the beautiful costumes on her Singer sewing machine, model 201K to be exact, which my sister Kelly now has as she inherited Mum's sewing skills and artistic flair. Kelly still uses Mum's Singer sewing machine today, which is now 60 years old and still going strong. They don't make sewing machines like that anymore. Mum would take her modern-day concert party, also called The Spotlights in honour of her wartime troupe, to various retirement homes, church halls, and the like to cheer up the less fortunate. The Spotlights were even asked to perform and sing carols at the Liverpool Town Hall by the mayor and lady mayoress on Christmas Eve one year. Gosh, how proud my mum was that day. God bless her.

My mum was very outgoing and everybody's friend. She was a beautiful-looking woman with striking features, blue eyes, and medium-short dark hair that she would curl for special occasions. Every week night, ten minutes before Dad came home from work, she would stop everything she was doing in the kitchen and go into the lounge room, sit down in her armchair, and bring out her make-up bag. She would open her compact and look into the little round mirror to powder her face. She would then apply black mascara with a small brush to darken her long eyelashes and use a black pencil to enhance her beautifully shaped eyebrows. She would paint her full lips red, which she would blot with a tissue. I loved sitting on the sofa, watching her go through her beauty routine, and she would always give me a playful wink at the halfway mark as she made herself more glamorous than she already was.

She always wanted to look nice for Dad. She would then go back to the kitchen to finish off our evening meal.

Dad would arrive home from work at the same time every night. He would put his pushbike away in the garage and come in through the back door into the kitchen, where he would give Mum a kiss and a cuddle and say, 'Hello, missus.' Mum's gorgeous eyes would flirt with Dad, and he was smitten.

All through their married life, like many families during those times, Mum and Dad scrimped and saved and tried their best to make sure we never went without, and my sisters and I grew up knowing the true value of money. Mum took charge of the household. She would budget Dad's weekly wage, paid all the bills on time, made clothes for us on her loyal sewing machine, and cooked us delicious meals seven days a week, all the while making sure Dad had an easy a life as possible after his horrendous time in Japan. They were so in love and depended on each other 100 per cent.

They couldn't afford to take us on holiday every year, but we did go to one of Britain's best known holiday camps once and had a wonderful time. The holiday camp was founded to provide affordable holidays for ordinary British families. Sometimes we'd go to Rhuddlan in North Wales for two weeks and stay in a caravan. We'd ride horses at the Pegasus Riding School, which was a short walk away from the caravan park, and play football in the field opposite the caravans. They were great times, and I look back on my childhood with immense fondness and gratitude for everything Mum and Dad did for our family.

A European holiday for our family was completely out of the question; that was until one of our neighbours, Mrs Murphy, decided to organise a coach trip to Montreux in Switzerland. She sent word out to the rest of the street, and it wasn't long before she had enough people to fill a coach at an affordable price for everyone. We were all so excited as, for working-class people like us, Europe was as far away and as unreachable as the moon. Mum took on another job, sewing curtains five nights a week in our front room for the cooperative store, and that money was put away each week towards our first European holiday. Sewing curtains would become a regular job for Mum as the co-op continued over the years with their successful 'buy your fabric here and have your curtains made up free' promotion.

Mrs Murphy's trip to Switzerland was so successful that a second one was arranged a couple of years later to Salzburg in Austria and then a third a couple of years after that to the quaint village of Saint Christoph in Austria. That was when I met Gustav. It was also when I met Mikael.

CHAPTER TWENTY-EIGHT

G USTAV WAS THE son of the owners of Hotel Matilda, where we had all stayed on our coach trip to Saint Christoph. We fell in love at 20 and kept in touch, visiting each other a couple of times. We lost contact along the way, but he was in for a big shock. It was twelve years later, and I was back in Saint Christoph.

Brooke and I had an uneventful train journey from Venice to Austria, which we were thankful for. We caught a taxi from the train station in Saint Anton to Saint Christoph, which was only ten minutes away. Saint Christoph am Arlberg, as it is officially known, is primarily a winter ski resort, like many Austrian villages. We were told that Saint Christoph became well known in the fourteenth century when a shepherd, Heinrich Findelkind, built an inn called the Arlberg Hospiz at the top of the Arlberg Pass, 1,800 meters above sea level, offering shelter and food to travellers and their animals. He knew the hazards and often deadly perils in crossing the Arlberg due to heavy snowstorms and inclement weather. It is written that seven lives were saved in the very first winter after he built the inn, and about fifty lives were saved over the next seven years. Sadly, the inn was engulfed in a fire in 1957 but was subsequently rebuilt and offers a whole range of wonderful amenities. It also houses one of the oldest wine cellars in Europe beneath the hotel. There's a lot of very interesting history surrounding the Arlberg Hospiz Hotel.

Saint Christoph is also famous for its warm Tyrolean hospitality and takes on a whole new dimension in summer, offering gentle walks and hiking, plus many other outdoor and indoor activities to choose from, in breathtaking and spectacular scenery. Saint Christoph is far removed from the hustle and bustle and is the ideal location for relaxing with loved ones. This beautiful small village is also close to other picturesque ski villages, with the city of Innsbruck, the capital of the Alps, only an hour and a half away by road. A longer drive to the Dolomites is also worth a visit.

We drove up the steep hill to Hotel Matilda. Memories of past holidays with my family came flooding back, and it felt like I'd never left this beautiful place. Everything looked exactly the same, with decorative wooden window boxes full of colourful flowers attached to the front of the pretty Austrian chalets. We spotted some locals walking around in their traditional attire, the females in short-sleeved white cotton blouses under waistcoats with flared skirts and clogs and the males donned in shirts with rolled-up sleeves under leather shorts with braces, socks up to their knees, and hiking boots, some with walking sticks and some wearing felt hats with a feather on the side.

When we arrived at the hotel, there was no one at reception, so we walked through to the cosy bar, where many a night had been spent socialising and drinking schnapps. I could hear the laughter of my mum and dad and the rest of the coach party, some of them getting up to tell jokes, some singing songs, and others just enjoying the frivolity of the evening. Nostalgia clouded my eyes, and I wished to God that I could reach out and pull the past back into the present.

Gustav's father, Hans, was behind the bar, and he looked at me as if he'd only seen me ten minutes ago. With a straight face, he asked, 'What do you want?' He always did have a dry sense of humour.

He went on, 'Gustav is married now with six children.' And while I stood there not knowing if this was one of his jokes, he couldn't hide that cheeky old smile of his any longer and came around from behind the bar and hugged me until I could hardly breathe. 'I'm only joking. Gustav is not married.' He laughed.

'And no children that I know of', he added with uncertainty.

I asked Hans if there was a twin share available, and if not, we'd try down in the village. Our luck was in. He took us up to a gorgeous room on the first floor, which overlooked the picturesque chalets, green hills, and ruggedly beautiful snow-capped mountains. The rooms at Hotel Matilda were absolutely charming, with timeless, traditional images of Tyrolean people and animals beautifully carved into the wooden furniture. There were enchanting photos of the Tyrol hanging in ornate wooden frames, underneath double-shaded wall lights. The beds were comfortable and inviting, with soft, fluffy duvets and pillows of the highest quality and luxurious white cotton sheets and covers, tempting all bodies to stay in bed until the end of time. In the hallway alcoves, there were locally carved religious figurines and poignant Tyrolean crucifixes hanging on white walls, stirring up emotions in the believers and the non-believers. The village church was chiming, and we felt momentarily pious, like we'd died and gone to beautiful Austrian heaven.

Hans casually told me that Gustav was running his own tavern down in the village now and gave us directions. After we'd unpacked, showered, and changed, we walked down the hill and into Gustav's bar and stood there, waiting to be served. I couldn't believe it was him, there behind the bar. After twelve years, I thought I'd never see him again, especially now that I lived on the other side of the world. I watched him serving the patrons, being the sociable and happy-go-lucky person that he always was, just like his father. Gustav was tall, around 185 cm, with dark brown hair and brown eyes. He was a good-looking strong man, and he was an expert snow skier, like most Austrians.

Gustav came over to take our orders, and as soon as he saw me, he nearly died from shock. 'No, it's not true,' he said, looking at me with complete surprise.

'Yes, it's true. I'm back *and* staying at your hotel.' I smiled, trying to appear nonchalant about it all but dying from excitement on the inside. He came around to the front of the bar, and we hugged for ages, both so happy to see each other again.

I introduced him to Brooke, and he escorted us over to a table, promptly telling his bar staff that he was taking a half-hour break. We chatted about old times, and he asked about my family. He was sad to hear the news of my mum and dad, recalling his fond memories of them not only from when we all holidayed here in Saint Christoph but in Liverpool as well when he visited me. He told me Mikael was still living in the village and still running his own bar. He told me they were friends now.

CHAPTER TWENTY-NINE

THE FIRST TIME I holidayed in Saint Christoph with my family and Mrs Murphy's coach party, I saw and fell in lust with Gustav, three days before I saw and fell in lust with Mikael. Well, I was only 20 and had all the correct and necessary hormones running through my body, so what was a young single girl to do? It wasn't that I played them off against each other; it wasn't like that at all, not really. I just spent time with both of them because I liked both of them; it was as simple as that. Neither of them knew I was seeing the other. That was until I was sprung by Gustav when he saw me leaving Mikael's chalet early one morning. He didn't seem too happy about that. Anyway, that was then. I was older now, although perhaps not necessarily any wiser, and you know they say history repeats itself.

'I have to get back to work,' Gustav said. 'But I'll see you later at the hotel, ja?'

'Great, see you there,' I replied.

After we left Gustav's bar, we stopped in at Mikael's bar, and there he was. He looked at me with total surprise on his face. 'What is this?' he asked. 'I don't believe it. What are you doing here? It's been so long.' He took me into his arms and squeezed the living daylights out of me. He looked the same, perhaps a little more mature looking. His blond hair was longer, and he'd grown a short designer-type beard. His deep blue eyes screamed mischief, and he still had the same cheeky smile on his lovely face.

'This is my friend Brooke from Australia. I live there now, and we're travelling through Europe up to London,' I told him. Mikael kissed Brooke on the cheek, and she gave me her wink of approval.

We celebrated our reunion into the early hours, with Brooke ending up behind Mikael's bar, serving us straight shots of rum. Of course, we didn't spend a penny, not that anyone knew we didn't have many pennies to spend.

During the evening, one of Mikael's friends, Gerhart, turned up. He was a traditional Austrian dancer and had arrived straight from his nightly performance, still wearing his lederhosen, long socks, and dancing clogs. He was so tall and handsome, and Brooke fell head over heels. 'Lucy, I'm in love with this man,' she said the moment she laid eyes on him. They made a gorgeous couple and didn't take their eyes or hands off each other all night.

At around three o'clock, after we'd all had more than plenty to drink, Brooke left with Gerhart, and I left with Mikael. I never made it back to our hotel that night, and it was hard to look Gustav in the eye the next morning when I got back. He knew where I'd been. There had always been this rivalry between Gustav and Mikael, and years later, it seemed they were still rivals, albeit healthy ones, which was good to see. I believe they now saw the humour in what had gone on years before between the three of us. It seemed this humour was required yet again as I made up with Gustav the next night.

Brooke and I were so broke that we could barely afford to eat. Fortunately for us, breakfast was included at Hotel Matilda, so we were able to fill ourselves up with fresh juice and pastries, bread rolls, cheese, butter and jam, and pots of tea. Lunch consisted of nothing, and dinner was soup and a slice of bread down at the village cafe each night. The later hours were spent between the two bars where we didn't pay for any of our drinks.

Brooke and Gerhart were certainly an item and were making the most of their time together after his nightly performances. I do believe that Brooke would have run away with Gerhart if she'd had the chance, and she still talks about him to this day. Gerhart absolutely adored her and made her feel cherished. She told me his lovemaking was not only romantic but also full of fire and zest, leaving her breathless just talking about it. 'I'm not sure if it's the altitude, Lucy, but there's definitely some sort of erotic magic in the air when Gerhart's around,' she'd say. She told me that he would literally take foreplay to another level, making sure her every need was satisfied. From what she told me, I seriously wondered if Gerhart had written his own edition of the Kama Sutra, leaving the man with the name starting and ending in *S* looking like an amateur. Lucky Brooke.

I was still an item with Gustav *and* Mikael in a ménage à trois kind of way, and the three of us carried on exactly the way it had been years before.

'Lucy, we desperately need cash, gorge. What on earth are we going to do?' Brooke was having a serious meltdown moment.

'I know, Brooke. I think it's time to put a call in to Barry to see if he can wire some money to us here in Saint Christoph,' I replied after some thought. Barry, my forever helpful brother-in-law, was back in Australia, and I knew he'd help. I made a collect call to him and gave him the details of the local bank.

'You girls just sit tight, and I'll wire the money straight away,' he said, extremely concerned that we were so destitute.

Each day after that phone call to Barry, Brooke and I would literally stuff our faces at breakfast in our hotel and then walk down the extremely steep hill to the bank to see if the money had arrived. Each day they told us it hadn't, so we'd walk back up the extremely steep hill and go back to our room where we would stay under the duvet covers, depressed and penniless, until nightfall.

Gustav told me the coach company that had brought my family and our neighbours all those years ago to Europe still brought holidaymakers to his hotel, and while we were there, one such coach party arrived. We met Bill, the driver of the coach company, the next morning at breakfast, and he instantly fell in lust with Brooke. We would sit at his table every morning for breakfast, and he would amuse us with stories of his many years as a coach driver. He was short, fat, and balding and, unfortunately for him, not the sort of look that rocked Brooke's world.

I came up with a plan that could well be the answer to our prayers. 'Brooke, if you flirt enough with Bill, mercenary as it sounds, it might just ensure our safe – and more importantly our *free* – passage back to London. What do you reckon?'

Brooke didn't look too enthusiastic. 'I'm not sure, gorge. What if he gets the wrong idea?' She cringed.

'Brooke, we're desperate. You said it yourself. Just give it a go. He loves you,' I replied with a wink.

Well, Brooke did flirt with Bill, which of course did backfire on her big time as he *did* get the wrong idea. Every time he saw her, he'd invite her back to his room, promising her the time of her life. She made excuse after excuse. 'Sorry, Bill, I have a migraine.'

'Sorry, Bill, I think I've eaten something that doesn't agree with me.'

'Sorry Bill, I feel queasy from the altitude.' Brooke wrote the book on excuses, yet not one of them could deter him.

Each afternoon when he got wind of the fact that we were in our room, after another one of her failed excuses, he would be knocking on our door, calling to her, 'Brooke, please just give me a chance to prove I'm worth it. You won't regret it, I promise.' He may have heard our muffled laughter coming from under the duvet covers. Towards the end of the second week, he made it known to Brooke that he wasn't a happy chappie, that she was flirting with him and not delivering the goods.

For days, I'd begged and pleaded with her to do the deed. 'Brooke, you have to sleep with him, if not for us, for queen and country – you know, that little old place we need to get to ASAP.' But she wouldn't succumb.

It turned out, however, that her flirting with him did eventually pay off in some small way. 'Lucy, you won't believe it, gorge. Bill has agreed to take us to the Swiss border.'

'And then what?' I asked.

'Well that's the thing – nothing,' she said, adding a despairing shrug. 'I was just chatting him up in the bar, even throwing in a hug and a kiss on the cheek for good measure. He said he couldn't take us all the way to England as the rest of the coach party had already started asking questions about us. He said they knew we weren't booked on the all-inclusive return trip, so that's the best he can do.' We both knew that he could've easily made up some cock and bull story to tell the paying travellers and taken us through to London if he'd wanted to, but a bruised ego was a hard one to mend, and his ego was well and truly black and blue, courtesy of Brooke – and myself for spurring her on.

Just before our two-week mark was up at Hotel Matilda, the money from Barry finally came through. What a long and drawn-out process that was back in the day! We asked for our bill and found that we were one day short in payment. We couldn't believe our continued bad luck; two weeks of waiting around for the money, and it *all* went on the hotel. We were back to square one – just as broke as we were the day we had arrived. We had thought that perhaps Gustav might have organised with his dad to give us some kind of discount, but it wasn't to be. Maybe the required humour Gustav needed twelve years on with regard to my still seeing Mikael was not as forthcoming as I thought. Ah well, I guess I deserved that one.

Gustav wasn't there that morning to say goodbye, and I never heard from or saw him again. Brooke and I were embarrassed enough as it was that we didn't have enough money to pay for the whole time we were there, and on the day we left, we put all the money we had in an envelope and left it at reception. We felt awful, but what could we do? Maybe it was just as well that Gustav wasn't at reception when we left. Mikael and I telephoned each other a couple of times when I got back to Australia, but that ran its own natural course.

CHAPTER THIRTY

THE COACH, WHICH by the way was only three-quarters full, was ready to leave, and Brooke and I were the last two to board. We easily found two spare seats and sat down amidst the hard-hearted glares and silence.

It didn't take long to reach the Swiss border, where Bill stopped the coach and announced to everyone that Brooke and I were getting off. Bill knew we were broke and didn't care one iota about how we would make it back to the UK. We even told him we'd pay the coach company in full when we got back once we'd found jobs, but he was having none of it. We disembarked, and he pulled our suitcases out from the luggage hold onto the set-down area. Everyone on the coach was whispering to each other and staring down at us, wondering what on earth was going on and why we were getting off in the middle of nowhere.

Bill got back on the coach, and drove off without so much as a 'goodnight, Vienna, and the best of British.' The particular Swiss border that Bill had dropped us off at was basically a passport checkpoint set up in the middle of a very long and lonely stretch of road. Brooke and I felt sick to our stomachs.

After we had our passports stamped, we dragged our suitcases to the side of the autobahn and just sat on them. We had reached an all-time low. 'Claire was right to leave when she did, Lucy,' Brooke said quietly.

'Yep, she sure was, Brooke,' I replied.

The two of us were unsure about what the universe was going to deliver up to us next, but Brooke and I were never down for long and always looked for the positive in every situation. After five minutes of sitting there, we decided that the only way out of this was to hitch-hike, even though we'd overheard someone on the coach talking about a female hitch-hiker who had been murdered en route from the same Swiss border only three weeks ago. What other options did we have? There was nothing else to do but pray.

CHAPTER THIRTY-ONE

B OTH MUM AND Dad had died six years earlier, just seven months apart, almost to the day, and it was a heartbreaking time for my sisters and me, to say the least. Mum had been complaining of severe headaches, culminating in a stroke which took our family by complete surprise, leaving us all in deep shock. She was taken to hospital, where it was found she had a brain tumour.

Three months later, the doctors decided to operate. We went in to see her the night before her operation. It was a Thursday because *Top of the Pops* was on television in the ward, and Mum was watching it. Strange, the things you remember. When it was time to leave, we kissed Mum goodbye, wishing her love and good luck for her operation the next day.

Devastatingly, her luck ran out, and our hearts broke into a million pieces when we were told that our beautiful mum never made it through the operation and that she'd died under the anaesthetic. She was only 59. We were all overcome with so much sorrow that life without her seemed impossible. Dad was grief-stricken, his eyes continuously red and bloodshot from crying every day after she died.

Dad had retired from the horrible tobacco factory, and to keep his mind active, he took on a part-time job. He bought himself a Yamaha motorcycle, pensioning off his pushbike after thirty odd years of reliable service. One fateful winter's day on his way to work, he lost control of his motorcycle on dry ice and ploughed straight into an empty concrete bus stop. He suffered a damaged spleen and other complications. He'd been a physically, emotionally, and mentally strong man all his life and would have most certainly survived had Mum been alive, but he missed her terribly. He was only in hospital for four weeks when he finally gave up. He died two days before his sixty-fourth birthday.

It was heartbreaking enough for us losing Mum, and now we had to deal with the emotional despair of losing Dad. Life couldn't have been worse for Kelly and me as we tried to come to terms with losing both of our wonderful parents and now having to live in the family home without either of them. Our elder sister, Elizabeth, lived three hours away with her husband, Barry, and their two young daughters, and they'd travelled up to be with us while Dad was in hospital. They'd organised Mum's funeral seven months earlier, and now they were organising Dad's.

Our dearly beloved Mum and Dad worked so hard all their lives and had given so much of themselves to family, friends, strangers, and people everywhere, especially people in need. It was just so sad that they never got to live out their well-deserved retirement together for longer. We were thankful that they'd shared a life full of love and that we'd all got to share some wonderful family holidays, not to mention the fun times we'd all shared in our family home.

Two weeks after Dad died, our gorgeous golden retriever, Paddy, died. Not long after that, our beloved cat, Sheena, died. We seriously wondered who was next. Elizabeth and her husband, Barry, were a great support to Kelly and me during those times, and we honestly don't know what we'd have done without them.

CHAPTER THIRTY-TWO

I HAD NEVER ASKED for my parents' help from the spirit world, but Mum, who believed in life after death, had said to me often during our talks on the subject that if ever she could help me from beyond the grave, she would. All I needed to do was to ask. I closed my eyes, and I prayed to the spirit world. *Dear Mum and Dad, if you can help Brooke and me, please help us now.* My prayer was short and to the point.

Ten minutes hadn't even gone by when a car stopped. A man who looked in his early twenties got out and came over to us. He was nice looking with a kind face, about 180 cm tall with brown curly hair. His name was Dieter, and he told us he was an off-duty policeman. *Oh no, please not another cop*, I thought. He showed us his ID and told us it wasn't safe to hitch-hike, confirming what we'd overheard on the coach that a female hitch-hiker had been murdered recently on the very autobahn we were on.

We told him our story, that we were broke and had been deserted in our hour of need. He seemed really nice and genuine. 'I'm on my way home to Basel. I can give you a lift if you would like.'

Brooke and I looked at each other, glimmers of hope written all over our faces. 'Thank you so much. That would be very kind of you,' I replied.

He put our suitcases in the boot of his car, and we were suddenly on our way to Basel with our saviour. I closed my eyes and smiled. *Thanks, Mum and Dad.*

As we were driving along, I desperately needed to go to the WC, so Dieter stopped at the next service station. I was almost peeing my pants and managed to get there just in time. Argh, the pain was indescribable. The burning sensation was sending shivers all through my body. *Oh no, anything else but please not cystitis*, I thought.

I sat there for ages until Brooke came in looking for me. 'Are you okay, gorge?' she asked.

'No, Brooke, I'm not, darl!' I wailed, telling her about my dire condition through the toilet door.

'Oh, Lucy, you've got honeymoon's disease, darl,' she said.

'I know only too well, Brooke.' We both kind of laughed. Payback time from Gustav and Mikael, I guess.

We got back in the car and hadn't even been on the road for five minutes when I had to go again. Dieter was amazing and drove as fast as he could to the next service station. I ran to the WC, but the door wouldn't open unless a coin was inserted to release the lock. Not having a Swiss cent to my name, I literally climbed over the top of the door, desperate to relieve myself, at the same time enduring the burning sensation that came with it. And that was how it was all the way to Basel, stopping at every service station along the way.

Dieter drove us to his parents' house who were away on holiday. 'You can stay here for the night,' he said. He made us a delicious pasta for dinner and told us to make ourselves at home and that he would be back the next day.

'Lucy, this guy is amazing. He doesn't know us from a bar of soap, yet he's actually letting us stay in his parents' house,' said Brooke.

'I know, he's unbelievable, Brooke. How lucky are we?' I smiled, knowing full well that help had been sent from above. Brooke continued to marvel at our unusual stroke of good luck. Dieter certainly was an angel sent from heaven.

Brooke and I shared his parents' bed when I wasn't screeching from pain for most of the night in the WC, yet despite such agonising discomfort from the cystitis, I felt that we were being looked after. I drank as much fluid as I could get my hands on, hoping to flush this awful thing out of my system. Poor Brooke didn't get much sleep either that night from having to listen to my cries of unendurable suffering for hours on end.

The next morning, a middle-aged woman came into the bedroom and, seeing us there, started screaming at us to get up and get out. It turned out she was the housekeeper, and no matter how many times

I told her, in German, that we were friends of Dieter, she wouldn't listen and literally threw us and our suitcases out of the house. I went flying across the polished floorboards, trying to get away from her, and sprained my ankle quite badly. So not only was I fatigued due to lack of sleep from an excruciatingly painful condition (and one that I wouldn't wish on my worst enemy) I was also now able to add limp to the list.

Brooke and I sat outside on the doorstep and waited for our angel to return. Dieter drove into the driveway and couldn't get out of the car quick enough. 'What is happening here? Why are you and your bags outside?' he asked.

'We don't think your housekeeper likes us, Dieter,' Brooke told him.

It was obvious he wasn't happy that we'd been thrown out. He went inside, and we heard a lot of shouting going on, mostly from Dieter. A few minutes later, the housekeeper stormed out of the house, muttering obscenities to us in German. 'Please come back in, and I will make us all some breakfast,' he said.

'Danke schön, Dieter,' I gratefully replied, and we went back in. We thanked him profusely for all he'd done for us and told him it was time for us to leave.

'How will you get to London?' he asked.

'Oh, we'll find a way,' said Brooke. 'We'll be fine.'

Dieter reached into his jacket and handed us something in an envelope. 'What's this?' I asked.

'Open it.' He smiled.

I ripped open the envelope and inside were two train tickets from Basel all the way through to Euston station in London. Was Dieter actually for real? 'Oh, Dieter, this is too much. We can't accept. You don't even know us,' I told him.

'No, please you must accept. You can send me the money back one day.'

Brooke and I couldn't believe it and thanked him again from the bottom of our hearts. As bad luck would have it, his address disappeared along the way. So, Dieter, if you happen to be reading this book, please send us your contact details so we can finally pay you back, that is, if you *really* do exist.

Brooke and I talked about Dieter many times over the years and how wonderful and kind he was to us. We would often come to the same conclusion that if ever we went back to Basel looking for him, we'd find that no one actually knew of him, that the local *polizi* had no record of an officer called Dieter, that his parents' house never existed and the wicked housekeeper had been a figment of our imagination, and that he really had been a spirit guide sent by my mum and dad.

Dieter drove us to the train station, flashed his police badge at the ticket collector, got onto the train with us, and lifted our suitcases onto the luggage rack. Once he'd made sure we were safely on the train, he stepped back onto the platform and waved us goodbye as the train pulled out of the station. Actually, I think Dieter must have been real because I still have the gold bullet he gave me as a souvenir from his police firearm, and I'm not sure that angels carry guns.

Brooke and I sat on the train and felt like the luckiest girls on the planet. Our mission in life to this day is still to pay Dieter back, plus interest for all the years that have passed since then.

CHAPTER THIRTY-THREE

THE TRAIN WOUND its way from Basel into France and up to Paris, the City of Love. We pulled into the main station, where we had to change train lines to get to Paris Gare du Nord via the Metro, the underground train system, to travel to London. The place was congested, alerting Brooke and me to stick together.

As we were approaching the turnstile at the Metro, there were three dashing young men, probably in their late twenties, walking beside us, conversing in French. They looked extremely suave, stylishly dressed in smart jeans, snazzy open-neck shirts, and expensive-looking jackets. All three of them had shoulder-length tousled hair, framing their high cheekbones and strong jaws, and we thought they had to be professional French models. 'Please, after you, Mesdemoiselles,' they requested, standing back, allowing us to go through first.

Mmm, drop-dead gorgeous and well mannered, I thought.

Brooke went through first, finding it somewhat of a struggle to get herself *and* her bags through the turnstile. Needless to say, the debonair models very kindly offered to assist. *Mmm, drop-dead gorgeous, well mannered, and helpful*, I harped on to myself. The guys were really friendly, chatting to us about how small the turnstiles were and that for the thousands of travellers that had to manoeuvre through them daily, they should have been made much wider. Mmm again as they spoke perfect English in their sexy French accents. Once Brooke and her bags were through, they assisted me with mine. It all felt so trouble-free having some kind broad-shouldered assistance, making us wonder how we'd managed to drag our luggage around all this time without it.

'Merci beaucoup,' said Brooke and I in unison after we'd bent down to pick up our cases, but they'd suddenly disappeared, lost in the madding crowd.

'Where did they go?' Brooke said, looking around, bewildered.

'Well, that was a quick vanishing act,' I added. We were both mystified by their sudden disappearance.

We carried on walking along the tunnel to our next platform when Brooke had an inkling that something didn't feel quite right. She looked in her shoulder bag and, to her shock and absolute horror, found that the zip had been undone, her purse, passport, and ticket to London from Dieter, along with Dieter's address, all stolen. Those gorgeous guys were professionals, all right – professional thieves. Talk about in the blink of an eye. We couldn't believe it – now what? 'Lucy, you wait here with the suitcases. I'm going to try to find those bastards.'

Just as I was about to protest about her going after them alone, Brooke had bolted. I felt completely vulnerable standing there in the middle of the tunnel with all our luggage, wondering who'd be along to violate me next and our remaining possessions.

I took the time to check my own bag, but nothing had been stolen, thank goodness. I'm sure they'd tried, but I always carried my bag across my body, which no doubt had made it difficult for them. Brooke normally did this too, and I think it was just this one time that she didn't for whatever reason.

Brooke was back within five minutes, her chase futile. 'They've gone, Lucy, gone with everything – my purse, my passport, my ticket, *and* Dieter's address. I honestly can't believe what just happened,' Brooke said, completely heartbroken.

We both walked back to the turnstile, only to find we couldn't get through as it was a one-way system for letting people out only. We had to call out to the ticket vendor to come over and release the gates so we could get back into the main station. Brooke explained what had happened, and he told us to go to the information office to report the theft straight away. When we got there, Brooke went inside while I waited outside. She'd been in there for less than a minute when she came back out, looking like she'd just been robbed a second time. 'Brooke, what's wrong?' I asked.

'Those pretentious pricks. The first thing I asked was, "Does anyone speak English in information?" And all they said was 'non' and then had the cheek to correct my pronunciation of *information*!' Pretentious pricks indeed.

I was so mad that I went in there myself where one of the so-called assistants behind the desk had his feet up on the counter. I stood in the middle of the floor and said in a very loud voice, 'Doesn't *anyone* speak fucking English in *inforrmat-see-on?*' The guys behind the counter just glared at me, not saying a word.

'Well, fuck off,' I said in an even louder voice. They scoffed as I walked out, but at least I felt better having got that off my chest. Talk about the City of Love. Paris had suddenly become the city of arrogance.

We were both beside ourselves with despair and didn't know which way to turn. 'We need to find someone who can help us and someone who can speak English. We need to find a policeman,' Brooke said steadily. We both shuddered at the thought, but we were in dire straits – again.

We dragged our suitcases through the busy train station, being pushed and shoved by all sorts of rude and impatient people. We hated Paris already and hadn't even left the train station. We finally found a policeman, who actually seemed interested in what we had to tell him; plus, he spoke surprisingly good English. It's a well-known fact that most Parisians *can* speak English; they just choose not to. Apparently, it has something to do with the war.

He took us to an interview room, where he called the Australian Embassy. He handed the phone to Brooke, who spoke to an official and told him what had happened. He told us to get a cheap hotel for the night, which they would pay for, and he made an appointment for Brooke to go in to see him the following day.

Well, we found a cheap hotel easily enough and one that looked for all the world like a bordello. Actually, thinking back, we're certain that it was. The woman who checked us in looked like the archetypal French madam. She would have been fifty-ish and was a real beauty. Her red hair was pulled up into a French roll, and her red dress was cut low at the front, revealing her large breasts. Her seductive emerald green eyes were heavily made up, and she had shiny red lips. She wore stunning antique-looking gold, ruby, and diamond drop earrings with a necklace to match. She had long red nails, and her elegant fingers were covered in gold and diamond rings which, we assumed rightly or wrongly, were gifts from her many lovers, and she was smoking a slim cigarette out of a black cigarette holder. Everything in the lobby was painted red. 'Hey, Brooke, we could always unpack our red dresses and earn some much-needed francs,' I joked.

'Lucy, don't, not even in jest, gorge,' Brooke replied, half-laughing.

Brooke gave the madam the phone number for the official at the Australian Embassy, whom she rang while we stood there, and he arranged for our accommodation to be paid for. We hauled ourselves and our suitcases into the rickety, cage-like old lift that took us up to the second floor. Our room was small and extremely basic, with a red bedspread, red velvet curtains, and pink floral wallpaper. There was a small chandelier hanging from the middle of the ceiling, which was quite elegant compared with the rest of the room. There was a wooden bedside table with a phone on it and some notepaper and a pen.

We both just looked at each other and started to laugh. In fact, we laughed so hard at our latest and greatest bout of bad luck that we thought we'd never stop. Of course, the double bed had a huge dip in the middle, so Brooke and I had no sleep whatsoever.

CHAPTER THIRTY-FOUR

THE NEXT MORNING at around eight thirty, tired and feeling like we'd had all the stuffing knocked out of us, we dragged ourselves downstairs to the breakfast bar for coffee and croissants, courtesy of the cherry-red brothel. We were swiftly roused by the decor and clientele when we got there and hadn't even slugged our first caffeine of the day yet. There was an old gramophone player behind the bar, together with a collection of Edith Piaf records. Full of raw passion, Edith's stirring, soulful voice filled the room with love, tragedy, loss, and pain.

There was one very long red vinyl bench seat with classic button tufting secured against the side wall, with eight or so small shiny brown tables positioned in front with ample room between each, enabling diners to chat privately. There were matching red vinyl armchairs on the opposite side of each table. There were three quite beautiful large crystal chandeliers hanging along the middle section of the ceiling, together with half a dozen or so bronze basket wall sconce lights illuminating this fascinating room. The walls were covered with gold damask-embossed wallpaper on a rouge background. There were large framed posters hanging up of French vaudeville characters, some in curious acrobatic poses, leaving nothing to the imagination. There were other large printed pictures of cancan dancers wearing revealing red dresses and feathered headbands in various dance poses, showing off their gorgeous legs and garters. There were other titillating, satirical-type posters of half-naked women showing their breasts, alongside villain-type leering men wearing black-tailed jackets, waistcoats, pants, and top hats, sporting interesting curled moustaches. We'd never seen a place like it in all our travels.

Brooke and I laid bets that the waitress who served us was the madam's daughter. She was very pretty and looked like she was around

25 to 30. She also had green eyes that were heavily made up, and her lips were full and red. She had shoulder-length auburn hair and was wearing a short black dress revealing almost the same-sized breasts as her odds-on mother, a white apron, black stockings, high-heeled shoes, and a garter. She placed a basket of warm, freshly baked croissants on our table, accompanied with brie and jam and the best French coffee ever, which she told us was bottomless. Yes.

The breakfast area was packed with men and women of different ages, the majority of them extremely alluring and bohemian looking, each of them moving with effortless grace and sensuality. It was such a sexually stimulating, arty-farty, showy place, and Brooke and I were absolutely enthralled, our eyes larger than saucers as we took it all in, loving every second. We took surreptitious photos of everything and everyone in the restaurant for those at home as evidence that we'd stayed at such a place. We felt like extras in some highly erotic French movie that was about to commence filming, and even though we were physically present on that lustful film set, the truth of the matter was that we were nothing more than mere observers on the outside looking in – actually, make that voyeurs due to the probable X-rated content.

We were wishing that we could extend our stay at the brothel to see what fun and bawdy happenings went on in the restaurant after dark. We spent an engrossing morning in this mesmerising hotel, but it was time to head to the Australian Embassy to plead Brooke's case. I do feel that had we stayed a couple of more nights here, this book may well have been a couple of chapters longer at the very least.

We arrived with time to spare for Brooke's midday appointment. While we were waiting to be seen, a young Australian guy on his way out stopped to talk to us. He told us that he'd found himself in a similar situation, where he'd had all his money stolen and had come to the embassy for help. He said he'd literally been interrogated by the embassy officials and that they'd made him feel like *he* was the criminal. He gave us some valuable advice, which was not to give up and not to leave until the embassy promised to help us as that was their job. Brooke and I looked at each other. 'That sounds ominous,' said Brooke. He wished us the best of luck and made a hasty exit.

'I think you're going to have to give a stellar performance, Brooke, after what our Aussie comrade just told us,' I advised her. 'You're going to have to convince them that everything that happened to you is the absolute truth, or they may not help us. You're going to have to cry.' Of course, Brooke laughed at that suggestion.

We'd been waiting for about half an hour when an Australian official came out of an interview room, calling Brooke's name. He asked her to follow him, telling me to wait where I was. After what felt like an eternity, the official came out to see me. 'Lucy, could you come in, please? Your friend Brooke is crying and is extremely upset,' he told me.

Good work, Brooke. I immediately activated my best concerned face ever and followed the official to where Brooke was. I rushed over and put my arm around her when I was asked by the same official to follow him into another room. I told the official that I was concerned about Brooke, not wanting to leave her, but he asked me again, rather curtly, to follow him. I wondered why he'd asked me into the room to see Brooke when I wasn't allowed to stay with her. It all seemed quite strange.

I was certain that he was asking me all the same questions he'd asked Brooke, obviously quizzing me to make sure we were both telling the same, truthful story, which of course I was. It was now close to three thirty when someone brought some sandwiches in and told me I could take a break, but I still wasn't allowed to see Brooke. Thirty minutes later, he resumed the interview. He went over everything for the second time to fully evaluate the situation and to reassure himself that Brooke's case was a genuine one. I was then taken into the room where Brooke was and told to take a seat.

'Do you know anyone in England who could send you some money?' he asked each of us. What on earth was this line of questioning about? It was almost like he was making one last-ditch attempt to see if we could help ourselves before the embassy did. I thought of an ex-boyfriend, Steve, who I knew would help. The official gave me a phone, and I rang Steve at work. It was a Friday night and the time in England was now close to five o'clock. Steve said he would go down town immediately and organise for some money to be sent to us. However, by the time he left work, all banks, travel agencies, and offices had closed. He rang the embassy back, apologising profusely that it was too late for him to do anything. Of course, it was the weekend coming up too, and everything would be closed until Monday. How times have changed.

The Australian official deliberated with his colleague, and only after fully satisfying themselves that Brooke had fallen victim to some serious bad luck did they agree to help her. He issued Brooke with a temporary passport and gave her enough money to purchase another train ticket, plus a little extra for incidentals. What an ordeal. Had they been trying to wear us down? Why had the Australian official been so hard on us? The advice given to us by the Australian guy on his way out rang true. We persevered, with Brooke also throwing in a few tears for good measure, and it paid off.

We left in a taxi and went straight to the train station, where we held on tightly to all bags, suitcases, purses, and passports. So much for our stay in gay Paree. Brooke bought her new train ticket, and we were finally on our way to Calais, where we boarded the ferry to Dover.

CHAPTER THIRTY-FIVE

T HE ENGLISH CHANNEL showed us no mercy, the ferry ride rough, to say the least. We heard fellow passengers spreading rumours of an imminent bomb threat to a channel-crossing ferry. Great. Not only were we feeling seasick; we also now had to live in fear of an explosion at sea and spent the next hour and a half praying that it was just a rumour. Terra firma couldn't come soon enough.

It was good to see the White Cliffs of Dover in the distance, and I wanted to sing Vera Lynn's rendition out loud from pure glee. The ferry docked without incident, and it never felt so good to be back on English soil. We boarded the train to Euston station, and it was there that Brooke and I parted ways, until we saw each other four months later back in Oz. We'd both decided that as soon as we arrived in the UK, we'd find jobs and work there for a while to earn enough money for our return trip to Oz. Brooke only stayed in London for a few days, bunking in with an old friend she used to work with, and I went to stay with ER, where I was reunited with my purse.

It wasn't that Brooke didn't try to find work; she did. However, as her original passport had been stolen in Paris, along with her right to work in the UK, Brooke had to think on her feet, hence an emergency call to her former boss, who was a successful management consultant with his own business, employing several office staff. He was also crazy and impetuous and was renowned for his fun yet eccentric behaviour. He was always up for a night out on the town and was over the moon to hear from Brooke. He promptly arranged a reunion at some swanky bar in town, inviting some of her old workmates.

Brooke had a brilliant night catching up with all the crew she used to work with. She was excited at the thought of working in London again and, of course, working for her quirky former boss. All was going according to plan when he started throwing strange questions at her, the strangest of which was asking her to go to Canada with him. Brooke hadn't seen him for a fair while, so why would he think she'd want to go to Canada with him? But this was the way he was, a spur-of-the-moment type of guy. Of course, Brooke had absolutely no intention of going to Canada with him, let alone anywhere else with him, except hopefully going back to work for him for a short time. Brooke laughed off his suggestions, like she'd done in the past, diplomatically steering the conversation back to him, giving her some work in his office, to which he agreed enthusiastically. But the icing on the cake, as far as the crazy times we'd experienced travelling through Europe together, was still to be delivered up to Brooke.

After a night of fun and frivolity with everyone, Brooke was ecstatic that she'd be back with the firm on Monday morning, earning some much-needed money. Brooke headed back to the office with her odd soon-to-be boss as he wanted to show her the fancy renovations he'd put in place since she was last there. As soon as they got there, he excused himself to go to the little boys' room. When he came back, he was looking somewhat dishevelled and wearing only his shirt – his jocks, socks, pants, and shoes nowhere to be seen. 'What are you doing?' Brooke asked, concerned about his state of undress, yet at the same time, not *too* overwrought by his predictable, peculiar behaviour.

'I think you know what I'm doing, Brooke,' he said, nonplussed, gamely showing her exactly what he meant.

'For the love of god, what on earth made you think that I'd want to do the business with you?' she asked.

'You know you want me, Brooke. You always did, so now here's your chance,' he continued, coming towards her with his unwavering, narcissistic, overinflated sense of self-worth.

Brooke immediately realised that he was now way out of control, more so than ever before, and from the look in his eyes, not to mention his overt, disgusting kinesics, no amount of sweet-talking was going to stop him in his tracks. She ran for the door, which was locked. She turned to him as he kept walking towards her. 'Just let me out now,' she demanded calmly.

He replied calmly, 'No sex, no job.'

Needless to say, Brooke replied, 'Well, you can shove your job in that case. Just open the door.'

He walked calmly back to where he'd left the key, walked back, and just as calmly unlocked the door for her. 'You're free to go, Brooke,' he announced casually. What an arrogant prick.

Brooke ran down the stairs and out into the London night, a free yet still penniless woman, appalled and upset by his weirdest outbreak of psychotic behaviour to date like she'd never witnessed before, not to mention all plans to work in London now dashed. Brooke knew he'd always had a soft spot for her, but it was the hard spot he now had for her that was messing with her plans. By the time she got back to the flat, she was shaking, the disgusting ordeal now manifesting itself through her whole being. She told her friend everything and urged her to warn all the girls in the office of his unhinged, disturbing behaviour. There were no other options available to Brooke except to ring Richard, cap in hand, who immediately arranged for her to fly to Fiji, where they had a romantic reunion.

CHAPTER THIRTY-SIX

I STAYED WITH EMILY for a few days, and she brought me up to date on her romantic antics with Yorgos. I thought how young and refreshed she looked. She told me that Ashley and Maggie were still full on with their holiday romances, and I was happy for all of them. Emily was already planning her next trip to Lindos.

I caught the train up to Liverpool and stayed with my old school friend Millie, whom I met at secondary modern school when both our respective schools merged. The first time I saw her in morning assembly, I thought she was the most beautiful girl I'd ever seen, and I wanted more than anything to be her best friend. She was 170 cm and had long thick dark hair which she always wore in a side plait. She had the biggest blue eyes and the longest eyelashes I had ever seen in my whole life.

Millie left school at 15 to pursue a career in hairdressing, while I stayed on until I was 16 to complete a commercial course. For my sixteenth birthday, Millie put five blond streaks in my long brown hair. Hairdressing was the perfect vocation for Millie. She was a Leo, and it was an understatement to say she loved a chat. Of course, we did become best friends; and when I told her I was coming back to Liverpool for a visit, she insisted that I stay with her and her parents while I was there. I ended up living with them for four months and worked for a temp agency, making enough money for my return trip to Oz. I loved being back in my home town and made the most of every second.

I caught up with Steve, who still felt bad about not being able to help us when we were in Paris, and I caught up with all my dear friends and relatives. I spent a fair amount of time at Billy Martin's dancing school in Old Swan, where I was taught to dance from age 16. My mum and dad used to dance there too. It was the most wonderful place where young, old, and every age in between went to learn ballroom and Latin dancing, and it was great to see Mum and Dad enjoying themselves.

I was initially dragged along to Billy Martin's dancing school by a girl I worked with at my first job after leaving school who said that everyone should know how to dance. On my first night there, I sat and watched in awe as everyone floated around the dance floor, making it look easy. When asked to dance the waltz by a nice young man and having to turn him down because I didn't know the first thing about dancing, I decided there and then that I would learn. I went to the beginners' dance class and loved it. From there, I joined the medal classes, where I attained my bronze, silver, and gold. Following on from my medals, I earned my Gold Bars I, II, and III; the Premier Award, and then the Laurel Award, the highest honour in the school, all with top marks. I had an amazing partner called Robert, and we entered a couple of competitions together, coming first in the Latin and second in the ballroom. Seven nights a week for years, I went there to dance, a place so close to my heart that I still go there in my dreams today.

Billy Martin, God rest his soul, used to tell me each night when I left at eleven, 'You should bring your bed.' And he was right. Even during office hours, all I could think about was ballroom and Latin dancing, even teaching my work colleagues dance steps in our lunch breaks. The senior partner, who had an office beneath ours, used to bang his walking stick on his ceiling, shouting, 'Keep the noise down!' They were such wonderful, fun times.

I visited my old family home and boldly knocked on the door. The new owners remembered me and invited me in to show me what they'd done to the place. I commended them on a first-class job, and I was happy the house was much loved, looking stylish, and no longer in dire need of maintenance. I felt extremely emotional and was overcome with soul-stirring, beautiful memories of the times my family and I had shared within those walls. After Mum and Dad died, Kelly and I found it hard to look after the house and garden. To be honest, our hearts just weren't in it; plus, we didn't have the money for the upkeep, so we reluctantly put our beloved family home on the market and immigrated to Australia.

I made an emotional visit to Mum and Dad's grave, where I laid fresh flowers and just chatted to them about stuff and thanked them again for sending Dieter. I told them I missed them every single day and that I loved them. I found it hard to leave their resting place as I didn't know when I'd be back. As fate would have it, it would be thirty-one years before I returned.

I finally made enough money to buy my airline ticket, left Liverpool, and headed back to Oz. I could, of course, write about some of the hair-raising times spent in Liverpool during those four months, but this book was only ever intended to be written about Brooke, Claire, and me and our adventures in Europe. As it turned out, due to the unforeseen circumstances, mishaps, and difficult and often dangerous situations we encountered along the way, our vacation in Europe sadly didn't amount to the full six months we'd planned for, even though I ended up being away from home for that amount of time. Brooke had already returned home to Oz after her two-week holiday with Richard in Fiji, and much to Richard's delight, they were a full-on item once again, that was until their next break-up. Claire stayed a further twelve months in Norway, earning big bucks in the fishing trawler business.

For years after our return, we would keep everyone amused for hours, telling our stories over and over again. For years too, my sisters, Elizabeth and Kelly, kept telling me that I should write a book about our escapades, and I did say that one day I would, and it would be called *Europe on a G-String*. It wasn't until years later when I was flicking through a magazine at home that I read my horoscope which literally said, 'If you're thinking of writing that book, now is the time.'

Oh my god, I thought, *the book!* Without further ado, I went straight into my home office, switched on the computer, and started typing. It was just one of those light-bulb moments as the memories came flooding back, and this book was the result.

CHAPTER THIRTY-SEVEN

A S I SAT on the plane returning to Oz, all I could think about were the amazingly unbelievable times the three of us had shared and the crazy situations we found ourselves in, and I smiled to myself. Our *Europe on a G-String* adventure had certainly brought with it many ups and downs, but I wouldn't have changed one second of it – well, perhaps a few nightmarish seconds, plus one that I definitely would have changed.

As soon as the plane entered Australian airspace in the early morning, I was consumed with feelings of absolute joy. The sun was rising, and I'd never seen the red earth below look so beautiful. Passengers were waking up to a new day down under, and I wondered what each person's story was. Perhaps some were on a similar journey to how mine started six months ago, venturing to the other side of the world, looking for new adventures and reasons to be alive. Maybe some were on emotional pilgrimages, visiting friends and relatives they hadn't seen in years. Perhaps some were on business trips. Maybe some were returning home, just like me. I was beyond excited to be seeing my family again and catching up with Brooke, and Claire when she returned home, to relive the crazy times we'd shared.

Not far out of Brisbane Airport, Peter Allen's song 'I Still Call Australia Home' was playing through the speakers of the Qantas 747, bringing a huge lump to my throat and tears of happiness streaming down my face. What a perfect ending to an amazing six months' journey. The words of the song said it all.

I was home.